ADVANCE PRAISE FOR *PLAY TO PROGRESS*

"To wean them from screens and engage them in three-dimensional, hands-on, body-on fun, these imaginative sensory-motor ideas are just what today's kids need. The activities will help them develop a sense of self, feel comfortable in their bodies, and grow to become confident, competent, 'in-sync' children."

—CAROL STOCK KRANOWITZ, M.A.,
author of The Out-of-Sync Child Has Fun *and*
coauthor of Growing an In-Sync Child

"Sensory play is a hugely overlooked foundation of healthy child development— physically, cognitively, emotionally, and socially. *Play to Progress* makes the neuroscience of sensory integration accessible to everyone, and is filled with creative and fun ideas for sensory 'nutrition' that helps kids feel and function at their best—and often sleep better, too. This book is an invaluable resource for parents, teachers, and anyone spending time with children."

—JENNIFER WALDBURGER, MSW,
cofounder of Sleepy Planet Parenting,
author of The Sleepeasy Solution

"*Play to Progress* presents plenty of fun, easy-to-perform activities that can strengthen parents' bond with their child and aid in their sensory development. Dr. Ticktin goes beyond merely presenting the exercises and delves into the 'why' behind sensory play and how it helps strengthen children's bodies and minds. In an age when kids are increasingly getting their sensory stimulation from screens instead of personal interactions, *Play to Progress* is a welcome reminder that there are many other ways to engage children's senses, and it can be a true pleasure for parents to share in those experiences."

—SHAUN GALLAGHER,
author of Experimenting with Babies *and* Experimenting with Kids

"I was lucky to meet Dr. Allie when my boys were just toddlers, and she quickly became my go-to resource for all things child development. I value her emphasis on good old-fashioned sensory development in an era when screens have become an all-too-tempting parenting crutch. Allie always offers simple solutions for engaging my children's senses without devices. I'm so grateful that, with this book, parents everywhere will be able to benefit from Allie's wisdom."

—CANDACE NELSON,
founder of Sprinkles Cupcakes and Pizzana

"This book is an absolute gem! Dr. Allie Ticktin has given parents and teachers a game-changing road map to empower children through open-ended sensory play. With compassion and skill, Allie walks you through the eight senses using insightful explanations of each. But more important, she offers a series of practical activities to engage your rigid, anxious, or distracted child. These tools allow you to meet your child where they are while creating play experiences that develop their individual sensory system. By helping your child better connect with their senses, they begin to engage more comfortably with the world around them—what a gift!"

—CAROLYN DALGLIESH,
professional organizer and author of
The Sensory Child Gets Organized

"Allie Ticktin is a visionary. She helped my wife and me become better parents. Her book will help you understand your child on a deeper level. The wealth of knowledge that she shares is practical, easy to do at home, and really fun. *Play to Progress* is the resource that every parent needs."

—STEPHEN CHBOSKY,
#1 New York Times *bestselling author of*
The Perks of Being a Wallflower *and* Imaginary Friend

PLAY TO PROGRESS

*More Than 90 Easy Exercises
and Activities to Develop
All Eight Senses*

PLAY

TO

PROGRESS

· · · · · · · · · · ·

Lead Your Child to Success

Using the Power of

Sensory Play

ALLIE TICKTIN, MA, OTD, OTR/L

Founder, Play 2 Progress

A TarcherPerigee Book

an imprint of Penguin Random House LLC
penguinrandomhouse.com

Copyright © 2021 by Play 2 Progress, LLC
Illustrations by Brian Lee
Photograph of the author by Dane Deaner

Penguin supports copyright. Copyright fuels creativity, encourages diverse voices, promotes free speech, and creates a vibrant culture. Thank you for buying an authorized edition of this book and for complying with copyright laws by not reproducing, scanning, or distributing any part of it in any form without permission. You are supporting writers and allowing Penguin to continue to publish books for every reader.

Most TarcherPerigee books are available at special quantity discounts for bulk purchase for sales promotions, premiums, fund-raising, and educational needs. Special books or book excerpts also can be created to fit specific needs. For details, write: SpecialMarkets@penguinrandomhouse.com.

Library of Congress Cataloging-in-Publication Data
Names: Ticktin, Allie, author.
Title: Play to progress: lead your child to success using the power of sensory play / Allie Ticktin.
Description: New York : TarcherPerigee, an imprint of Penguin Random House LLC, 2021. | Includes index.
Identifiers: LCCN 2020055868 (print) | LCCN 2020055869 (ebook) | ISBN 9780593191927 (hardcover) | ISBN 9780593191934 (ebook)
Subjects: LCSH: Perceptual-motor learning. | Sensory stimulation. | Play. | Motor ability in children. | Senses and sensation in children. | Child development.
Classification: LCC LB1067 .T54 2021 (print) | LCC LB1067 (ebook) | DDC 370.15/5—dc23
LC record available at https://lccn.loc.gov/2020055868
LC ebook record available at https://lccn.loc.gov/2020055869
p.   cm.

Printed in the United States of America
1   3   5   7   9   10   8   6   4   2

Book design by Patrice Sheridan

Some names and identifying characteristics have been changed to protect the privacy of the individuals involved.

Neither the publisher nor the author is engaged in rendering professional advice or services to the individual reader. The ideas, procedures, and suggestions contained in this book are not intended as a substitute for consulting with your physician. All matters regarding your health require medical supervision. Neither the author nor the publisher shall be liable or responsible for any loss or damage allegedly arising from any information or suggestion in this book.

PLAY TO PROGRESS

CONTENTS

Introduction

SENSORY SUCCESS

. . . .

From the moment they are born, children explore the world around them and begin to discern what is happening inside their bodies by using their senses. That input helps them get to know their surroundings, develop their gross and fine motor skills, and understand themselves. When they play, they are noticing how the dirt feels under their feet, their speed through the air while riding a bike, or how cold the ice cream is as they take a big lick, all of which nourishes their sensory system and teaches them how to engage with their environment. The sensory system develops as they interact with the world. In fact, for kids, perhaps the most meaningful way of experiencing the world is through play. Play has the power to lead our little ones to become children, and eventually adults, with the confidence and skills to chase their dreams.

If a child constantly wore mittens, they would have difficulty developing the fine motor control of their hands and fingers that they need to be able to pick up small objects, handle a crayon, or play games. If a child was never given the opportunity to physically explore their environment, it would be challenging for them to learn to move around and interact with others. In fact, studies have shown that children who spend their early life without sufficient sensory stimulation—in this case because they lived in orphanages—are physically and cognitively behind their peers.

These are extreme examples, of course, but the reality is that when a child's sensory system is not nourished, they may be at a disadvantage that can manifest physically, academically, and socially. I see it all the time in my work as an occupational therapist at my company, Play 2 Progress, where we help children build skills for the journey through childhood using the power of play. We see kids who struggle to stay seated during circle time, participate in a sport, navigate the classroom, build a structure out of blocks, write their name, copy from the board, or—what I find to be the hardest to see—develop a positive self-image and make friends. The bad news is that, in my experience, it's only getting worse. In recent years, I've seen multiple infants whose parents, with only the best of intentions, have placed them in equipment that is marketed as great for babies but can actually delay development and lead to difficulty sitting or walking. What those little ones really need is what *we* had—tummy time, an opportunity to move, and the freedom to develop their muscles. I've also seen children who were thought to have ADHD because they have trouble concentrating in school, when the real reason they fidget and move constantly is that they don't have the postural control to sit in a chair. The good news is, if your little one is struggling with a sensory challenge—maybe they are a picky eater or are afraid of heights (we all have something)—it can be overcome. How do I know? I've seen sensory success both from my professional vantage point as an OT and from overcoming some sensory challenges of my own. The best way to do it is by doing something your kids already love: play.

We have eight senses (yes, eight!), which are responsible for processing the information in our environment, making sense of it, and informing us about our body and surroundings. If your child throws a ball toward a target but misses, their sensory system will provide the feedback that they need to modulate the force and throw softer or harder on the next try. This type of trial and error is as critical to their growth as a healthy diet and a loving home.

I often think of a little girl named Heidi, whom I met in the early days of Play 2 Progress. Heidi's mom came to us in tears because she had just received a call from her preschool that since starting school the month before, Heidi was not adjusting well and had not connected with a single other child. Heidi would hang on the edge of the playground, find a corner, and watch the other kids play, but she never joined in. When I met Heidi and brought her into the sensory gym, the first thing I noticed was that she was not exploring at all. I decided to bring her a puzzle, and we sat on the ground to play. That was when a new Heidi emerged; she was chatting away and telling me about her pets. As it turned out, Heidi was oversensitive to her feet leaving the ground, which we will explain later in the book, and she was a bit clumsy. She wasn't playing at school because the other kids moved too fast for her and the play structure was scary to climb. After our work together, she loved the swings and was ready for the kindergarten playground when she started school the next year.

It likely won't surprise you to hear that our kids are increasingly entertained by gadgets and placed in high-tech pieces of equipment that smart marketing convinces parents they need, starting within the first few months of their lives. When we put our babies in Bumbos and Jumparoos, it pulls them out of their natural movement patterns and places them in developmentally inappropriate positions, which both creates poor posture and is completely passive, not allowing them to strengthen their muscles. A Jumperoo can actually *delay* a child's ability to walk, or promote toe walking and impede their physical development. In short, overusing equipment sidesteps a baby's ability to develop naturally, engage their sensory system, and freely explore, which is their number one way of learning about their environment.

I am passionate on this topic because we are all constantly fed ads for these items, which can be detrimental to a child. Remember, the best place when it comes to your baby's development is on a mat in a safe place on the floor. We want them to constantly be engaging with the world. I wrote this book to help you understand that there are dozens of ways to activate their sensory system and give you ideas for play.

• • •

There are a few scenarios that I hear about all the time from my clients, and they might sound familiar to you, too. The sun is shining, and Ashley is enjoying the day as she drives to pick up the most important people in her life from school, knowing that this calm will soon turn into chaos. Lyla is right behind her in the carpool line. Indeed, as soon as the kids pile into their cars, they fight for attention. Lyla's five-year-old, Jack, wants to play on the iPad when he gets home, and her seven-year-old, Ivy, wants to play video games, while Ashley's five-year-old, Tyler, asks to turn on the TV in the car, and her two-year-old, Lola, begs for her mom's cell phone, which she has used effortlessly since she was twelve months old.

Ashley turns on music to try to distract the kids from their demands and asks them to notice how nice the weather is, but their requests escalate into loud demands. Lyla tries to play "I Spy" to no avail.

After ten minutes of whining, Ashley tells the kids that she will decide, based on their behavior for the rest of the ride, what they can do once they get home and have a snack. (She knows that they will *not* be playing video games tonight, but she can't handle that fight right now.)

Lyla settles for a little friendly competition—whoever is able to stay the quietest will win one extra bedtime book. Ivy loves to read and manages to make the least noise, so she will get an extra story tonight.

At home, Ashley realizes that she is out of dino nuggets. She has alphabet nuggets in the freezer, but they're a no-go for Lola, who makes the average picky eater look like a gourmand. As panic creeps in, she asks her daughter if she would like to try the alphabet nuggets, but Lola refuses. She agrees to a small bag of Pirate's Booty, while Ashley worries absentmindedly that Lola hasn't been eating enough protein. Tyler and Lola sit at the table with their snacks.

Over at Lyla's, Jack refuses to come to the table. In between bites, he jumps off the edge of the couch or runs around the kitchen island pretending to be a ninja, always one kick away from a broken dish. Ivy goes running because she can't handle the loud noises that Jack makes every time he crashes into something.

Her face dusted with the remains of her popcorn, Lola requests her favorite cartoon, *Peppa Pig*, and Ashley reminds her that there is no *Peppa* on school nights. Instead, she shows Lola the app for learning shapes that she downloaded on her iPad; it is marketed as educational, but it looks like a game. Lola heads to the playroom with the iPad. Ashley turns her attention to Tyler, her Energizer Bunny. His laughter constantly echoes throughout the house—he seems to have only one volume, and it is *loud*—and he has been known to send Lola running when he comes at her with his arms wide open for a hug. Tyler doesn't realize how strong he is and squeezes her until she screams. Ashley knows he would benefit from burning off some of that energy outside, but with a small yard, there aren't many options and he quickly gets bored of chasing the soccer ball. When he requests *Paw Patrol*, she agrees to let him watch for a few minutes. She feels slightly guilty but knows the TV will occupy him.

Lyla has to get laundry done and finish a project for work. Jack's teacher recently mentioned that he is having trouble recognizing his letters, and she would like to sit down and work with him on that, but she needs every minute she can get. Rather than working through the alphabet with him, she downloads an app that teaches letters and gets him settled at the table next to her, iPad in hand, while she turns to her project.

• • •

We all know that we should cut down on screen time—for ourselves as well as for our children. I no longer look twice when I see a baby in a stroller at the park, zoning out on a cell phone instead of looking at the trees and listening to the sounds around them. Concerns about screen time, which is associated with decreased white matter—the connective superhighway of the brain—and lower cognitive skills have not escaped the notice of pediatricians. One recent study that was striking, even to me, concluded that children "who used screens more than the recommended one hour a day without parental involvement had lower levels of development in the brain's white matter—an area key to the development of language, literacy, and cognitive skills." With that said, reducing is really hard to do—more and more these days.

Let's face it: raising kids can be exhausting. In the chaos of daily life, screens keep them calm and occupied while parents race to meet deadlines, get dinner on the table, and entertain their family. You see screens in restaurants, parks, airports, and even schools. Our kids no longer learn the skill of attention in a crowded restaurant when, instead of crayons, they are given an iPad and are not expected to engage with their family or their own imaginations. But here's the thing: while a digital tablet may mesmerize children and even keep them out of trouble, it won't engage their sensory system—and that's a big problem. Parents want what is best for their little ones, but screen time is abundant in our world, and while they know it isn't ideal for their kids to be staring at screens in the house, at the table, and in the car, they don't know what else to do.

Don't get me wrong. Screens have a time and (limited) place in our young ones' lives. FaceTiming grandparents or taking a virtual kids yoga class are great, but we want to try to limit passive screen time, when nobody is interacting or moving their body. And I don't want you to beat yourself up if you need to shower and the only way to do that is by turning on a twenty-minute show for your child to watch; we just want to balance out that passive time with more movement and engagement.

Long gone are childhoods like mine, and probably yours, that meant spending every minute after school outside until sunset. If it was sunny, we were running around barefoot; if it was raining, we'd be jumping in puddles. If we had given much thought to it, we would have said we were just hanging out with our friends or playing games, but we were actually strengthening the building blocks of our sensory system that contributed to us becoming doctors and artists, receiving a full ride to college on a baseball scholarship, or having the passion for working with children that allowed me to become an occupational therapist.

Although they may not be playing around outside, children are *busy* these days. Most of my clients are typical kids with overly scheduled lives. In fact, starting in kindergarten or even preschool, most of them do not have a single day of the week without a scheduled activity. Their parents often ask me about whether playing sports can make up for a lack of physical movement during the rest of the day. I tell them that sports are great for the sensory system and learning to work as a team, but that time is still highly structured and doesn't permit outside-the-box thinking or imaginative play. Our little ones must have time for free play, too.

Let's go back to Ashley and Lyla. Each of their kids needed something that they weren't getting; instead, they were all placed in front of a screen. Jack is struggling to write his name and learn his letters, and last week his teacher asked Lyla to practice with him at home. An app may assist him in memorizing the shape of each letter, but it would be much more effective for him to use his hands and learn through his sensory system. When children are having a hard time with writing, it helps them to use tactile items to make the letters. Jack could form letters out of Play-Doh, shaving cream, or sticks. He could get the letters wet and explore their shapes using more than rote memorization, all while using his tactile sense. Stimulating the sensory system on multiple fronts is an infinitely more effective approach. It builds neural connections so kids can learn about the world, think abstractly, complete complex activities, acquire language, master gross and fine motor tasks, and interact with others.

As for Lola, who, at two years old, is a natural at using her mom's tablet and cell phone, she is not able to complete a simple stacker or shape puzzle, as most kids her age can, and Ashley thinks she seems a little clumsier than her brother. With two kids under six years old and two parents working full-time, the truth is that Lola has received less one-on-one attention than Tyler, and it is often the path of least resistance to hand her the iPad, especially at a restaurant or in the car. When Ashley took her to the park last weekend for a birthday party, she realized that her daughter did not know what to do. She was not climbing on the structures like her friends or exploring her environment—instead, she was running around aimlessly. Ashley tried to get her to play with a few toys that the other kids had brought, but Lola doesn't seem as creative or interested as her peers. Ashley began to worry.

Not only that, but Ashley recently had a concerning parent-teacher conference about Tyler. She and her husband get a kick out of his energy and how he loves to high-five everyone in sight, but this is causing problems in pre-K—the other kids run away when he approaches, because, like his little sister, they don't like how hard he high-fives them.

Flash-forward five years. Lola is seven, in first grade. She's the smartest kid in class, but she's, well, awkward. She struggles to make friends and isn't interested in sports or other physical activities. She is a messy, picky eater who refuses to try anything new. Every morning is a battle to get her to school, and Ashley thinks it's because the playground is so stressful for her to navigate.

Tyler still has a hard time sitting in one place. He's a sweet kid and a strong swimmer, but his teachers are constantly calling him out for his behavior and he is beginning to think of himself as a bad kid. Ashley has noticed that he is becoming more disruptive, too.

Jack keeps up in class, but he has poor penmanship and just

doesn't seem to like academics, which is a surprise and a bummer, because Lyla remembers how curious he was as a toddler, a little sponge taking in everything he encountered.

If we told our grandparents that we had to teach the new generation to *play*, they wouldn't believe it. But preschool teachers tell me that it's become a big part of their jobs, and their students don't know how to enjoy free time without toys that light up, make noise, and play *for* them. Kids need to learn how to engage with the objects in their environment and with their peers to be prepared for kindergarten. If you are a teacher or educator, you have likely seen this struggle, and there are many activities in this book that you can adapt to the classroom to encourage hands-on sensory play. (See page 55 for ideas on how to set up your classroom in a sensory-supportive way.)

Ashley's and Lyla's stories may seem extreme, but I see families like theirs on a daily basis, in my office, at their homes, and in their classrooms. At Play 2 Progress, we guide children and their families through proper development using both a nurturing environment and the right level of challenge.

No two kids are the same, and there is no single reason why a child behaves the way they do, but when I watch a child play from the sidelines of their preschool classroom, I can see the areas of their sensory processing that may need strengthening or attention where a teacher or parent may see acting out. One of my four-year-old clients, Johnny, loves to karate chop, squeeze, and roll on his friends. His teachers had been using a variety of behavioral strategies, without much success, to teach him that these behaviors were not OK. When I assessed him, the first thing I noticed was that these actions were clearly making him feel good and that they helped him feel calm so he could sit and learn in circle time. He was karate chopping his buddies not to be mean but because his body needed heavy work to self-regulate and calm down. "Heavy work" is any movement that pushes or pulls on his muscles. Unfortunately, not only were his relationships taking a hit, his teachers were constantly calling out his name for making trouble. It's hard for a four-year-old to understand why he's hearing "no" for doing something that his body needs so badly, and he was coming home from school upset.

Fortunately, I was able to work with his teachers to turn Johnny's situation around. By providing him with socially appropriate ways of getting heavy work—through activities like the ones in this book—we helped him to better understand his body. When Johnny felt the need to squeeze, we guided him through using easy statements, saying something like, "I can see your body really likes how that feels. It's OK if your body needs squeezes, but it isn't OK to get those squeezes by squeezing a friend, but why don't we try rolling a weighted ball on your legs instead?" This shifted the conversation from "We do not squeeze, that is not OK, keep your hands to yourself," and essentially shaming him, to empowering him and helping him to understand what he could do to make himself—and his classmates—happy.

Bottom line: a child cannot learn to navigate the world without playing. We need imaginative people, out-of-the-box thinkers, who can find solutions to everyday problems, whether that's building a bridge, solving medical mysteries, or starting a business. Abstract thinking, self-confidence, and social awareness—each of which starts with play—are vital, and they are formed and developed when we engage a child's sensory system. The question is, how do we play with children to do so?

This book will walk you through each of our eight senses, explain the role of each, and give you a series of activities to engage it. Don't skip ahead—it is important to read and understand what each sensory system does and how it works. They don't operate in isolation—all the senses work together—so while a given activity may be directed at nourishing a particular sense, most will draw on more than one to encourage your child to strengthen various areas, from fine motor to athletic skills.

There is not a set length of time or number of days that you should try each activity. Use this book as a building block—a starting point for how to play in a sensory-supported way. If you are doing scooter board hockey (see page 37) and it turns into scooter board dancing, let it happen! Play is never rigid. If you like an activity but your child would rather play princesses, or pirates, or pirate princesses, then go with the flow. The most essential thing to remember is that these activities should not feel like homework, and each provides endless opportunities and possibilities for your child to use their imagination. I hear from many parents that they don't actually *know* how to play with their children, so as you become more comfortable letting loose with these activities, you'll tap into your creative inner child, too.

Each activity, while aimed at ages three to eight, also suggests ways to make it more challenging or a bit easier so you can meet your child where they are. If they are struggling with a particular exercise, feel free to dial down the difficulty (or try something else). Once your little one has mastered a skill, level up and make it more ambitious. You can come back to an activity again and again as your child gains proficiency or a game becomes a go-to favorite. Each child will have a different response to a new sensory input, so make sure to watch their reactions and behaviors closely. Tyler may be able to handle lots of stimulation, while Lola becomes easily overwhelmed and needs to start slowly. You never want to push your child to a place of discom-

fort, so ease them in. This is especially important for the big movements in the vestibular (balance and spatial orientation) section;
vestibular input is extremely powerful, and children can experience a
delayed response like dizziness or a tantrum even if it seems like they
are enjoying it. Always watch and wait for your child's cues before
continuing with any activity.

Let this book be your guide in learning about and understanding
the sensory system and engaging with it in ways that your child has
never done before. My ultimate goal is to get your kid playing—
playing with you and playing with tactile, tangible, pliable items that
allow for creativity. It's the best way to help their brains and bodies
grow.

Let the fun begin!

1

THE SENSORY SYSTEM

· ·

Nothing is more important than our children. If you're like most parents I know, you've spent untold hours up late fretting and searching for support on the internet about everything from nursing to sleep. You've quizzed your pediatrician and bombarded friends and family with questions about what to expect. At the heart of all this concern is what every parent wants: a happy, healthy child who is hitting their developmental milestones.

Newborns are bombarded with input from the moment they are born, and kinesthetic activities and physical play are critical to strengthen their sensory system and get them ready for preschool—and life. Although we can continue to improve our sensory system over the course of our lives, the sweet spot for laying the groundwork for success is birth to age five. And there is a lot you can do for your child during this time period because the sensory system plays a role in everything your child does. We'll discuss the eight senses of the sensory system at length, but for example, a toddler uses their tactile system to explore the texture of their food, their proprioceptive system to bring that apple slice or sweet potato to their mouth, and their vestibular system to remain sitting upright while eating. Likewise, an older child playing with clay needs to maintain their posture (vestibular) and feel the texture of the material on their hands (tactile). Their smushing, pulling, and molding is the heavy work that provides proprioceptive input.

Given the barrage of sometimes-contradictory information out there, parents can become obsessed with what is "normal" as they watch their child learn and grow. Often, parents focus on what their little one is *not* doing rather than celebrating the incredible changes happening right before their eyes. Yesterday they weren't rolling, and today they are easily avoiding tummy time. But rather than being in awe of this little human who has been in the world for only a few months, too many of us frantically turn to Dr. Google because the baby is only rolling to the right and not to the left. What if we shifted from wondering, "Why aren't they rolling to their left?" to considering, "How can I help them learn to roll to the left?" A strategy like placing a favorite toy on the left may do the trick.

There are similar opportunities to aid our children in conquering each breakthrough (largely through play) until they are ready to trade in their childhood bedroom for a college dorm room. The problem is, no one is teaching these basic strategies and games, so many parents feel at a loss for what to do. Naturally, they turn to the latest technology that claims to enhance their child's development; before long, their kids are spending hours "learning" from an app rather than by interacting with the people and things around them using their senses.

Most crucially, kids need to develop a sense of self—*this is where I am in the world*—to feel comfortable in their bodies and self-assured when they connect with others and interact with their environment.

Children who can move with coordination in the space around them have more confidence and have a solid sense of where they are physically, are better able to enter into unfamiliar territory—a new classroom, playground, or activity—and can then more thoroughly participate and interact with others.

Not too many years ago, these developmental skills came to fruition naturally in the yard, neighborhood, playground, or living room. But increasing time pressures, as well as safety concerns (here in LA, most schools no longer have swings in the yard), mean that many kids have not had the opportunity to explore their surroundings in a way that we all took for granted.

So how is a time-strapped parent supposed to balance the daily realities of an overbooked life with what is best for their kids? Trust me, I get it—it can seem overwhelming to do play "right." There is a way, however, to develop their sensory system. But first, let's dive in to understand what the senses are and what they do.

The Eight Senses for Success

When most people are asked to list the senses, they think of the big five we learned in elementary school: sight, hearing, taste, touch, and smell. When it comes to the sensory system, there are three more: movement (vestibular), body awareness (proprioception), and internal awareness (interoception). Your child needs all eight senses working robustly to help them grow to their fullest potential.

THE SENSORY SYSTEM

· · · · · · · · · · · · · · · · · · · ·

Vestibular: Processes movement and balance; coordinates the motion of your head with your eyes; involved in bilateral coordination, postural control, and level of physical arousal.

Proprioceptive: Provides feedback on where your body is in space; controls the force and pressure of your movements.

Tactile: Allows us to distinguish between qualities of touch (i.e., light touch, prickly, soft); recognizes pain and temperature.

Visual: Allows us to process and make sense of the items we see in our environment.

Gustatory: Supports our ability to taste and identify the five flavors: sweet, salty, sour, bitter, and umami/savory.

Olfactory: Allows us to distinguish between different odors and decide if they are safe and pleasant (flowers) or dangerous (smoke); connects to our emotional system, bringing back memories (the most famous example, of course, being Proust's madeleine).

Auditory: Allows us to not only hear but to discriminate and interpret sounds to allow for an appropriate response.

Interoception: Tells us what is going on inside our bodies; lets us know when we need to go to the bathroom or are hungry or thirsty.

We'll delve into each sense one by one, but as you can see from the following diagram, all aspects of the sensory system work together to build a foundation for the abilities and skills children need to be successful in everything from self-esteem to academics to sports. Our senses are like tree roots—if they are strong, then the trunk and branches will also be strong, but if these roots are not nourished, a child may not be able to become their best self. In other words, a well-developed sensory system builds the foundation that allows other skills and abilities to develop and flourish. Our goal here is to develop a strong sensory system, i.e., the roots, using play from the time a baby is born. And even if your child is struggling in one or many of these areas, the activities we'll discuss can put them back on the path toward mastery.

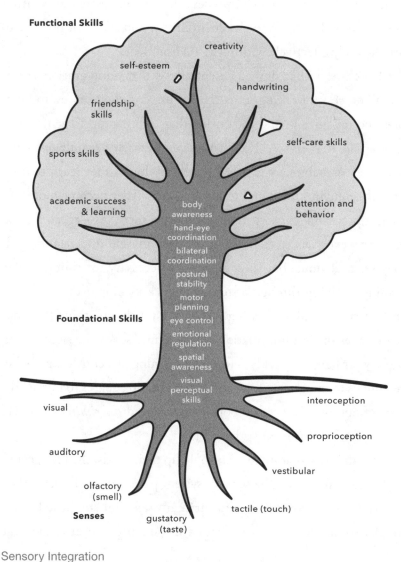

Sensory Integration

What Is Sensory Integration,
and Why Is It Important?

Jean Ayres, an occupational therapist who studied extensively on the sensory system and developed the theory of sensory integration, defined it as "the neurological process that organizes sensation from one's own body and from the environment and makes it possible to use the body effectively within the environment."

Let's break that down. Essentially, sensory integration is our brain's process for taking in feedback from our eight senses, to interpret and organize it, and then using that information to generate an appropriate response. As I've mentioned, we rarely use only one sense at a time. As babies are exposed to sensory input, they learn to decipher their environment and to respond to it. They become more efficient at processing sensory input as exposure increases—meaning that each new experience creates fresh connections and understanding. It may seem obvious, but these senses are necessary for riding a bike, reading, walking through a store without knocking over the display shelves, sitting still, and eating. When you touch something hot, your brain takes in that information and instantly sends the signal to remove your hand—quickly—from the burning object. Most activities require us to integrate information from multiple senses to initiate the correct output. We need to both *modulate* and *discriminate* (we will dive into what this means a bit later).

We all know that infants first hold up their heads, then roll, crawl, and eventually walk. The sensory system plays a crucial role in their ability to plan movements and maintain postural stability. For example, some kids have a difficult time staying still at circle time because they physically cannot sit crisscross applesauce for twenty minutes. When a child struggles with praxis—the ability to formulate an idea for what they want to do and then make that plan happen— they may also have a hard time with motor planning, appearing clumsy and uncoordinated.

A child's brain is like a sponge, ready to absorb everything they see, feel, and taste, and establish connections that they will use for the rest of their lives. Those associations are developed from the kind of experiences you get from playing in the backyard with friends, running around a playground, or reading a book.

So, what happens when kids aren't exposed to a variety of sensory input, and most of their playtime is spent with electronic toys and gadgets? In short, they may not process the information they come across as efficiently. Kids need back-and-forth interaction, which happens in play when they do something and another child or adult responds. As I say to parents, watching kids play and interacting with them should be like watching a tennis match, with a lot of back and forth. Play is not passive.

I often say I found my passion for working with kids through my childhood love of playing with baby dolls. A child who enjoys building with a LEGO set or blocks may become an architect; another who is skilled at sports could go on to be a personal trainer or coach. It's not always such a straightforward correlation, of course—and it's not about directing your child down a particular lane for the rest of their life—but it all begins with play. The reality is kids are engaging in free play much less than when we were kids. But the cost is dear, as they lose the ability to be creative, play, and socialize.

It's not just kids who have lost the magic of play and become caught up in overscheduled lives. I'm no longer shocked when parents tell me that they don't know how to play with their children. One client was concerned about their child, who didn't seem to be interacting with the other kids on the playground. Sometimes they played with LEGO sets together at home, but they didn't play any imagination-based games and they didn't try any physical activities. If you're stumped about where to start, know that you're not alone, and there are plenty of games and activities in these pages to inspire you. Unlike when we were kids, many parents today don't let their kids play outside alone anymore, which is one of the easiest ways to stimulate their sensory system. That loss means that it's important to be thoughtful and deliberate about play and the toys you give your children. At the same time, I encourage parents to let themselves be silly and enjoy themselves, too.

Before we get to the fun stuff, let's explore those eight senses and learn how to foster them. As I've mentioned, remember that although we'll talk about each sense in succession, they rarely (if ever) work in isolation. In everything we do, we integrate multiple senses to interpret what we are experiencing and issue a proper response. In addition, for every sense, we want a child to be able to *discriminate* (for example, telling the difference between hard and soft) and to *modulate* (meaning to have the "just right" response, neither over-reacting nor under-reacting) to sensory input.

Sense 1: Vestibular

You may not have heard of the vestibular sense, but you use it constantly. This system is all about movement. When you move, the fluid in your inner ear does, too, which is detected by the otolith organs and semicircular canals, which sends a message to the brain about head position and tells us where you are in relation to gravity, as well as your speed and direction. It is also our system that allows us to balance. When your little one is walking along the curb, the vestibular system, along with the proprioceptive and visual systems, is helping to keep their balance.

Sense 2: Proprioceptive

The proprioceptive system gives feedback about where the body is in space and controls the force of movements. Receptors in muscles, tendons, and joints communicate about the position of the muscle and its amount of tension, which then controls the force response. It gives a child the body awareness that lets them bring a Cheerio to their mouth or hold a crayon without breaking it. Along with the vestibular system, proprioception is most closely associated with motor planning and coordination.

Activating proprioception has a calming effect because it helps to self-organize and regulate our responses to other inputs. An infant using a pacifier is getting proprioception through their mouth to help them calm. After stimulating the vestibular system by spinning on a swing, bringing a child's energy up, proprioceptive work like pushing a toy car through sand or carrying something heavy helps a child to calm (which is especially useful before bed- or naptime).

Sense 3: Tactile

Our touch receptors relay information to keep us safe, impact our emotions, and give us information about the pressure, location, and qualities of a physical stimulus, like whether it is painful or pleasurable, the temperature, and information about our movement.

The tactile sense is another component in sensory-integration and one of the many senses we discuss at Play 2 Progress. (In fact, "sensory" has become a bit of a buzzword these days. You can find ideas all over Pinterest for containers filled with rice and little items for kids to discover.) We want to give children many opportunities to explore their environment through touch, by allowing them to get messy and really dig in—without grabbing the baby wipes every few minutes.

Sense 4: Visual

The visual system uses light waves that enter our eye and form images via our cornea, pupil, and retina, eventually reaching the brain's visual cortex. It gives us the ability to process and make sense of what we see, whether that's a photo of a parent or a favorite color of crayon.

Sense 5: Gustatory

Our taste buds distinguish between five flavors (sweet, salty, sour, bitter, and umami or savory), which are interpreted in the brain. Make sure to expose your kids to a variety of tastes from when they are young (and even in the womb) to diversify their palate and avoid picky eating. If a child has never been exposed to a particular food or taste, they are likely to reject it later on.

Sense 6: Olfactory

Airborne odor molecules are processed by your olfactory receptors in the nose and interpreted into what we know as smells. This system allows us to decipher those smells as pleasant, like a flower, or alert us to danger, like the smell of smoke. Our sense of smell is connected closely with our memories, which can evoke strong emotional responses. It is key to keep this in mind when thinking of your child, because scent can be a powerful tool for calming them down. Babies and toddlers often attach to a lovey (a blanket or toy), and if you've found that a replacement of the exact same item won't do the trick (or that it gets rejected after being laundered), that's often because it is the smell of that lovey that is comforting.

Sense 7: Auditory

You know this one. The auditory sense takes in sound waves, which produce small vibrations in our inner ear, which are then sent to the brain and interpreted as the sounds that make up language, music, and noises of alarm that guide us through daily life. The auditory sense also allows us to discriminate what we are hearing in order to generate an appropriate response. If we hear an ambulance while driving, we know to pull over to the shoulder, and when children hear a bell on the playground, they line up to go inside.

Sense 8: Interoception

This last sense isn't talked about as much as it should be. In short, interoception is our understanding of what is happening inside the body, which helps children identify when they are hungry or full, and when they need to go to the bathroom. It also influences their ability to identify their emotional state as anxious or frustrated. Kelly Mahler, the author of *Interoception: The Eighth Sensory System*, describes it as answering the question "How do I feel?"

If a child has a tummy ache, they need to recognize that the butterflies are because they are nervously anticipating a sleepover. This is key when it comes to general mindfulness about their body. If a child is having trouble with interoception, then potty training, regulating eating, and even staying calm is difficult.

• • •

We all have sensory differences: Does your partner like the TV so loud that you find it distracting? Do you have a co-worker who stands just a little too close when they talk? Do you have trouble sitting at a desk for a long period of time or feel a constant need to fidget? These small distinctions are common among adults, but if a child isn't given the opportunity to fully and regularly use their sensory systems, they may experience more significant challenges as they journey through life. The good news is that just because it is essential for their development doesn't mean it can't be enjoyable.

Before You Play

In the next chapters, you will learn more about each sense and also get to the fun part—the activities—and I'll give some general pointers about making your time with your child as enjoyable and engaging as possible. But first, a word or two on play, play spaces, toys, and how sensory input can have an impact on your child's self-regulation (their ability to manage their emotions and responses to their environment).

A child's environment can have a big impact on their temperament. To avoid overstimulation, there are a few things to keep in mind when you set up their room or play area. First, I recommend that you keep toys out of your child's bedroom entirely. Their bedroom should be a calm space with soothing colors and very few items on the walls. It's wonderful to have a few books on hand for bedtime, but try to keep everything uncluttered and cozy. It should be a safe place where they can relax their bodies and rest. When a child has toys in their room, they are often tempted to play with them, and it becomes a room for play rather than a room for relaxation and sleep. If you don't have a playroom or have limited space, I suggest devoting a corner of your living room to toys. If that sounds overwhelming, don't worry: it doesn't have to look like a cluttered toy store. In fact, having very few toys out at a time is best.

I was recently at my client Aaron's house, and from the minute I walked in, I noticed a long trail of toys. I followed him into the living room, which is where I assumed most of the toys were kept, as evidenced by three overflowing baskets and a few bigger play pieces strewn across the floor. So, I was surprised when Aaron said, "Let me show you my playroom." At that point, I began to panic. Then I saw the playroom. It looked like a tornado had deposited toys on every surface and in every corner. Between the two rooms, Aaron easily had over one hundred toys. No wonder he wouldn't play with one for more than thirty seconds. How could he? Whenever he had a tantrum, he would start throwing toys, which made perfect sense to me—the sheer number of them was incredibly overstimulating.

Because of this and similar experiences, I have started going into my clients' homes and doing playroom edits. In my parent talks, I always bring up just how necessary it is to have fewer toys for a child to choose from, and whenever I specify a maximum of ten on display at once, eyes begin to pop. If your child has too many options, it will be more difficult for them to sit with any one toy for a longer period of time because they are constantly distracted by the others. Over the years, I've seen firsthand just how overstimulating most play spaces can be. (See page 111 for setting up your space for sensory success.)

Keep things simple: minimalist and clean is the way to go. A fantastic option is to have a toy storage closet—or a storage container under the bed, if you are short on closet space—and rotate the toys between stored away and out to play. When your little one gets sick of the ten that they have to choose from, exchange them for ten different ones (it's like having a birthday every few weeks).

Not all toys are created equal. If you have ever been in one of Play 2 Progress's Parent & Me classes, you know just how much I believe this. As technology gets smarter and more prevalent, even the regular old toy aisle is rife with the latest technology. Today's toys light up, quack, roll, make noises, and play *for* a child rather than allowing them to use their imagination to roar like a lion or make the train move by pushing it along the floor. It's better to offer toys that your little one can actually play with rather than toys that operate on their own. In fact, research shows that engaging with basic toys—meaning toys that don't have an electronic or digital component—promotes an increase in language among children as well as in parent/child interactions.

You may not be surprised to hear that my preferred option is an old-fashioned wooden toy, whether that's a car or an animal or a kitchen set. (Bonus: they look much classier than a plastic contraption and will make your designated play area more stylish.)

I suggest building a calm corner in one area of your house. You can use a small teepee tent or an area that is going unused, just big enough for a child to crawl into, like between the arm of the couch and the wall. Keep this corner very simple and try to limit the amount of light and noise coming into the space. Don't put anything inside except for a cozy blanket and a weighted stuffy. It is important to never direct your little one to the corner or make it feel like it is a punishment or time-out. Instead, this should be a safe space that they go to when they need a break. Build it together, and talk about it as an option for whenever they need to feel calm.

Each sense, used in different ways, can either help your child calm down, like before bed, or wake their body up, like for a day at school after a sleepy morning. For example, fast swinging will wake your child up, while a soothing massage will help them settle into bed. We will dive more deeply into this in each chapter, but here are a few brief suggestions.

At Play 2 Progress, we call helping a child to calm down, whether from a tantrum or from having too much energy, "getting back into the green zone." This is a term from a program called the Zones of Regulation, which is popular in many schools and the sensory world (and the perfect addition to every home). It is a handy tool for all children to understand how their level of arousal and emotions relate to their bodies. At one time or another, all kids get frustrated or angry over anything from wanting to continue playing when it's time to stop, to feeling overwhelmed emotionally (when parents leave for a date night) or physically (overtired), and need some support to get reset.

The techniques we use at Play 2 Progress often use heavy work, which we will describe more in the proprioception chapter, and emotional strategies to help kids regain a sense of control over themselves and their emotions. Here is what we show parents to guide their little ones as they come down from a tantrum.

GETTING BACK INTO THE GREEN ZONE

- Validate their feelings in one sentence:

    I understand that is upsetting . . .

    I see you are very sad . . .

    Wow, this is so hard. You really wanted that [toy, ice cream, etc.]. You must be really disappointed. I understand . . .

- **Let them know that you are there for them and love them.** Let them know that if they need a hug, they can come get one.

    I can see you are really upset right now. I am going to give you some space to calm your body, but I love you, and if you need a hug, you can come get one.

- **Give them space, and do not talk to them too much.** Be a pillar of support without using verbal language and instead rely on body language. Speaking will only further dysregulate them.

- **If there is an item that helps them calm (a weighted stuffed animal, a lovey, etc.), place it in their vicinity (so they can see it), but** do not hand it to them directly. Let them come to it on their own.

- **Offer them space, and wait it out with them.**

- **If they grab something unsafe (like scissors), gently take the object and in a calming voice say,**

    I want to keep your body safe, so I am going to take the scissors.

- **Once they calm and come to you, do not rush to make them clean up any mess they made while tantruming or make them apologize;** instead, simply reassure them that you love them. Let them fully calm, and then continue to wait. After you have given them some time, you can talk about cleaning up, moving on to an activity, etc. Wait longer than you might think before this step.

- **Do not shame them for tantruming or continue to talk about it throughout the day.**

We want to turn to calming sensory inputs to help ease the body into relaxation. It is important to limit bright visuals or loud noises (as well as your talking) and instead move to a room with low light and minimal sensory input. Try deep pressure from a massage or a weighted blanket, slow rocking or swinging, deep hugs, lowering the lights, drinking warm milk or water, sucking on a pacifier or water bottle, and listening to white noise or a child-appropriate meditation. Teaching your little one to breathe to help them calm down is also a great strategy that they will carry with them into adulthood.

On the flip side, some kids need to help their body wake up. We often focus on how to get a child to calm down and forget that some kids struggle with increasing their energy level—often in order to pay attention in class. For this, we turn to sensory strategies that are alerting. It may be easy to understand how swinging, which is vestibular input, increases energy levels, but we can also draw on the other senses here. For example, my best friend recently reminded me that before standardized testing in Michigan, where we grew up, the teachers gave out peppermints. Licking a raw lemon, smelling peppermint, playing games that are fast, listening to loud music, turning on bright lights, touching something that vibrates or is really cold, and eating crunchy snacks are all activities that will wake up a child.

I often think of a client of ours, Jayson. Jayson, who was in first grade, was known around school as the child who was always tired. He would lie down at his desk and skip recess, and often wouldn't laugh or get silly with his friends. Jayson's perceptive teacher had a feeling that his low energy level had to do with his overall sensory processing and sent him to us. When Jayson came into Play 2 Progress, we put him on a swing and provided him with different types of intense sensory input. By the end of our first session, we noticed that he had begun to talk and engage much more easily. Jayson began moving his body every day before school, bringing lemon essential oils with him, and taking movement breaks throughout the day to stay alert, engaged, and regulated.

If the information a child takes in from their senses feels like too much or not enough, they may not even have the words to tell you how they're feeling (remember, they don't yet have a baseline for what things should feel like!), and they may feel out of control or unsafe in their body. It's as if their flight-or-fight impulse is on red alert and they can't pay attention to anything else. To get an idea of what this is like, imagine that you and your partner are en route to a long-awaited vacation. You arrive at the airport and discover that you can't find your passport. If your partner chooses that moment to ask where you want to eat when you land, you naturally won't be able to focus on that question and may, well, freak out. When a child's sensory system is on overload, they can calm themselves down by engaging their senses through play (and using the sensory inputs that help them feel calm). One thing I always like to mention is that a child who is not regulated will have a really hard time learning, because you need to be regulated in your body to be an effective learner.

Getting Ready to Play

I've grouped the sensory-building activities by sensory system, with additional fine motor and gross motor exercises at the end of the book. Under each activity, before the directions, you will find a list of the materials, the space you need, and how much time it requires. I have also provided ways to make the activity either easier or harder as needed. Children have a wide range of abilities, and it is important that you adjust your expectations based on their skill level. These activities are best for kids who are about three to eight, but a six-year-old may be challenged by something a four-year-old does with ease. Don't push if your child struggles with an activity; you can always go with the easier version or try something else. Tailoring our games to what an individual child can accomplish is something we do constantly at Play 2 Progress. Finally, I have included some Baby Bonus Activities to get your littlest ones engaging their sensory systems, too.

Setup is straightforward. I suggest choosing a designated area for play, whether that is the corner of your living room, at the kitchen table, or in a playroom. A number of activities will be messy—making them even more entertaining—so have an old towel for covering up the play space and wear clothes that you don't mind getting dirty. You don't have to do every activity or even do them in order. However, I encourage you to try a few from every chapter so that you make sure to engage all the senses. Please note, too, that although each activity is listed under a particular sense, it may involve other aspects of the sensory system, because most play engages more than one sense. For example, jumping on a trampoline provides both proprioceptive and vestibular input—the act of bouncing up and down triggers force against muscles (proprioception), and the inner ear responds and adjusts to that movement of going up and down (vestibular).

A Word on Safety:

1. Make sure you have an open area without furniture or other objects with sharp edges. Some of the activities require balance and coordination, and we want to keep everyone intact!
2. Wear a helmet while on anything moving (e.g., a scooter board).
3. Make sure you are using nontoxic, child-safe art materials.
4. Some items are choking hazards, so keep them out of the reach of small children.

5. Pay attention to your child's cues. The sensory system is sensitive, and we don't want to overdo it.

Skip around in each chapter and find the activities that you and your child like the most and that fit your space and time requirements. Although all the activities are "good" for any kid aged three to eight, this is meant to be fun and enjoyable, so if it ever feels like homework, move on to another.

A few more guidelines and rules of thumb when playing with your kids in general: Try to put your phone down and turn it to vibrate or silent, even if it is only for fifteen minutes. I know that can be hard to do with work constantly buzzing on the line, but even fifteen minutes of one-on-one attention can go a long way for a child. My final suggestion is to channel your inner five-year-old. Yes, that means getting silly. I often see parents hesitate to let go, worried that they will embarrass themselves, but I promise, it will be cathartic for you as well. Show your kids how play is done, and they will play right back. Together you will create a beautiful moment and not only strengthen your bond but get them on the path to success.

MEANINGFUL MOVEMENT

Moving the Body to Engage the Vestibular Sense

. . . .

The vestibular sense is one of our most important senses because it bolsters our relationship with gravity; that is, it lets us know the position of our head while we are moving. It impacts balance, posture, self-regulation, and coordination. All children need to engage the vestibular sense to develop properly, to sit upright and copy from the board, to bounce a ball, and to eat their lunch. Any activity that requires coordinated movement involves the vestibular system in some way.

How the Vestibular System Works

The semicircular canals and otolith organs in the inner ear are sensitive to movement and feed information to the brain about where the body is oriented (upright, lying down, moving). That information allows us to respond appropriately to our environment, to maintain

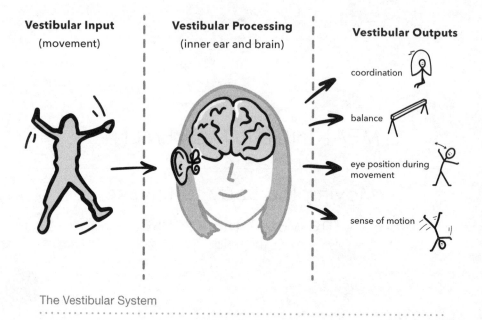

Vestibular Input (movement)	**Vestibular Processing** (inner ear and brain)	**Vestibular Outputs**
		coordination
		balance
		eye position during movement
		sense of motion

The Vestibular System

balance, and to coordinate our movements. If you have ever had motion sickness or an inner ear infection, you have an idea of what it is like when the vestibular sense is not working in sync with the rest of the body. You may have felt dizzy, unsteady on your feet, uncoordinated, or unwell.

We are largely unconscious of the vestibular system when it is working properly. We don't think about what it takes to ride a bike, catch our balance, or do a somersault. Children need to stimulate their vestibular system on a regular basis so that they can build their relationship with gravity and comfortably participate in a variety of movement.

As with all the senses, children need opportunities to develop and strengthen them, and they do this largely through play. The more experiences they have (and the more fun they have while doing them), the better their vestibular sense will operate. Because it is a critical part of the sensory system, even infants benefit from vestibular activity and can get it through rolling over or being rocked gently.

The vestibular sense will help a child to feel secure as they move through the various environments and activities they're likely to encounter in a day, from sitting at the dinner table to climbing on a jungle gym to joining a game of jump rope. When a child has a solid sense of their relationship with gravity—especially when their feet leave the ground—they have increased confidence in being active, playing, and moving. This sense of self-assurance expands to other areas. If they are confident in how they move, they will feel confident about themselves in general. They will be quicker to join in at recess, more likely to be perceived by their peers as outgoing and a leader, and will have a better sense of self.

In a classroom, the vestibular sense allows the eyes to track easily from one object to another, moving from the teacher at the front of the room to a paper on their desk without having to make major adjustments or head movements. It lets them maintain their gaze even when their head is moving, like a ballet dancer doing pirouettes all while looking at a fixed spot. The vestibular sense contributes to attention and regulation—being able to maintain the correct level of arousal. It also contributes to hand-eye coordination, which is essential for sports and writing.

If children do not have a well-developed vestibular sense, then they may be working so hard to sit upright in school that they can't fully pay attention to what a teacher is saying. They may fidget and move around in an effort to stay seated at circle time or in their chair, leading to reprimands. Can you imagine *needing* to move, your body unable to hold your posture for an entire lesson, only to get in trouble for following that instinct? Those regular scoldings can deeply impact a child's self-esteem.

They also may have trouble playing games with friends or participating in sports, missing out not only on fun but on friendships and teamwork as well, which can likewise be a blow to self-confidence. Being able to skip, kick a ball, or do a cartwheel may seem unimportant to an adult, but a child who has trouble with these activities may not be included on the playground. A lack of belief in their physical abilities may make them hesitant to join in, so they often end up playing alone. A healthy vestibular sense supports a child's independence in many ways, contributing to the skills required to read aloud from the board, bend over and tie their shoes, and play tag with friends at recess. The confident kids on the playground are often the most coordinated.

A child with a well-developed vestibular sense—among other senses—will be able to adjust their behavior and transition from big movement to quiet time without a problem, like when they have to switch gears from being active on the playground to settling down in the classroom. (On the flip side, if they aren't able to get through those transitions because the movement caused them to become dysregulated, it can lead to tantrums or distraction.) They will be more successful in school, enjoy play, and be better able to interact with friends, family, and the world around them. Other benefits include:

Arousal level: Just-right arousal is necessary for sitting still at circle time, paying attention, socializing, problem solving, and learning, and vestibular input has a big impact. Gentle vestibular input like slow rocking can be calming, while intense vestibular input like spinning can often increase a child's energy level to what some parents may describe as hyper. Some children become dysregulated, and when a child who is dysregulated becomes disruptive, teachers may label them "bad"—and, sadly, the child often takes that characterization to heart.

Vestibulo-ocular reflex: This reflex stabilizes the gaze when the head and body are moving, whether that's while dancing, dribbling a basketball, or copying from the board. Being able to hold a steady gaze or chase a ball while running assists a child as they navigate safely and successfully through their environment—at home, in the classroom, and on the playground.

Coordination: I have mentioned how the vestibular system impacts coordination because of how our relationship with gravity impacts our awareness of our position in space and movement. At Play 2 Progress, we also look at bilateral coordination, which is the ability to use both sides of the body in a coordinated manner. It's necessary for the arms and legs to work in sync while riding a bike, climbing stairs, getting dressed, and playing sports. In school, a child needs bilateral coordination to write, cut a piece of paper (one hand holding the paper and one hand using the scissors), and draw.

If a child struggles with their relationship to gravity and they are not grounded or confident in their body, they may feel out of place and awkward, which directly influences their confidence level and self-esteem. When a child is uncomfortable in their body, their behavior can be expressed at either end of the spectrum: they can be disruptive and unable to sit still, or they can be shut down and quiet. The withdrawn child is often overlooked as not needing assistance because they behave "well" and do not cause problems in the classroom, but they need attention just as much as their more disruptive peer.

Core and postural strength: The core and postural muscles—the muscles in the back, abdomen, and pelvis—are necessary for playing sports and games and sitting still and upright, whether that's on the floor in circle time or in a chair at meals. The vestibular system has an impact on the overall tone of the postural muscles that help us work against gravity, and it stabilizes our head to maintain our posture. This means that if a child is standing or sitting still (like in line for the potty or in circle time), these muscles keep them upright.

Our vestibular system does not work alone. Our proprioceptive system also contributes to overall posture. Without good postural control, a child may get in trouble for leaning on a classmate or furniture, or lying down at circle time. They also may move around frequently to adjust and correct their posture, which can be distracting for them, as well as for other students, and get them in trouble. Some of these kids seem like they are in constant motion.

Balance: Balance refers to the ability to maintain one's center of gravity while moving—up, down; left, right; forward, backward. Balance is a key component of all movement and activities. It is a key ability for social play, whether that's unstructured playground activities, kicking a ball, or being able to compete in sports.

Key Aspects of the Vestibular Sense

Vestibular discrimination: A child who struggles to differentiate where they are in relationship with gravity (upright, slouching, tilted) and how fast they are moving will have trouble in daily life and in the classroom. They might move much faster than other kids, unaware of their speed because they are unable to feel whether their body is going fast or slow. If they trip, they may not be able to sense in which direction they are falling, not catch themselves, and break their arm. They may also appear clumsy.

Vestibular modulation: Modulation is all about finding the just-right response to a sensory input. We don't want to have too big or too small of a response; instead, we want a response that matches the sensory input appropriately. Think of "Goldilocks and the Three Bears"—we want the just-right response. When a child does not have the appropriate response to movement, they may be afraid of physical activity or fearful of allowing their feet to leave the ground—so they won't jump, swing, or climb, and they're so cautious that it impacts their ability to play with other kids or enjoy the playground. This child is what we call over-responsive to vestibular input. To them, their feet leaving the ground feels terrifying.

Another child may need to move more than other kids to find a just-right level of arousal. This is what we call under-responsive. They may appear lazy, lethargic, and unmotivated to get up, but once you get them on a swing or jumping around, the difference in their energy level becomes clear. That is because they need more movement than the average child to be energetic and engaged in whatever is going on.

A child can also crave input. They may be more active than other kids or act impulsively, with a lack of safety awareness as they spring off the couch and over the table. Circle time, grocery shopping, and any task that requires them to sit still is tricky; they can never get enough movement because they are constantly craving vestibular input.

Vestibular Activities

These activities can be alerting (energizing), so it is important to not let kids get too wound up doing them. This alerting effect can "wake up" a child who is less active and who tends to slump, have lower energy, or lean against objects for support. If they do seem overexcited, try a proprioceptive activity (see page 61) to calm them down and allow them to get regulated. They can also have a delayed impact, meaning that a child may feel the effects after the activities are over. (If you have ever been on a Scrambler at an amusement park, you may have felt fine on the ride and immediately after, but you then got dizzy several minutes later.) So take it slow, check in with your child to see how they are feeling, and stop if they are not comfortable in any way. Look to their body for cues—they may not be able to verbalize their experience. They may be dizzy or nauseated, or their energy and behavior may become "too much" or "hyper."

Finally, because vestibular activities require movement, be sure to clear the space where your child is playing so they won't bump into furniture or other objects.

Downward Dog Coloring

1+2   3+4+5   (optional)

Description: This game, which develops creativity and fine motor skills, keeps children occupied and having fun. Kids of all ages will love it.

Materials:
- Chalk, crayons, paint, or markers
- Paper

Space: Small

Time: 5–15 minutes

Setup: Place a large piece of paper and coloring utensils of your choice on the floor.

Directions

Step 1: Position your child in a shortened downward dog (feet about shoulder-width apart and bent at the waist for their hands to reach the ground, making a V-shape with their body) or a wide-legged forward fold.

Step 2: Place the paper and the crayon or marker about three inches in front of your child's hands.

Step 3: Have your child place their nondominant hand on the floor.

Step 4: Then, have them pick up the crayon or marker with their dominant hand.

Step 5: Begin coloring, and watch them create their next masterpiece!

Make it a little easier: Take frequent breaks and alternate between coloring in downward dog and while lying on their tummy.

Make it a little harder: Place the coloring utensils about one foot in front of your child. Ask them to keep their feet planted and to walk their hands forward to get the coloring utensil and then walk back to their original position. This will work on core strength because they will be walking their hands into a plank position in order to reach the coloring utensil.

Baby Bonus Activity: Put paints inside a Ziploc bag, add glitter if you like, and tape it shut. Place your baby in tummy time and let them use their hands to move the paints around in the bag.

Additional Skills: Proprioceptive, Fine Motor

Potato Sack Rolling Race

1   2+3   4

Description: Rolling not only brings out the laughs, it also supports the development of the vestibular system. It is possible for your child to get a bit too dizzy with this one, so watch their cues and take breaks as needed.

Materials:
- Potato sack or body sock
- Small balls or beanbags
- Bucket or laundry basket
- Timer (optional)

Space: Large

Time: 10–15 minutes

Setup: At one end of your race area, place a pile of balls, beanbags, or other small portable items. On the other end, place a bucket or a laundry basket.

Directions

Step 1: Have your child get inside the potato sack or body sock.

Step 2: Let them choose an object that they will take with them to the other end of the race area.

Step 3: Have them lie on the ground and then roll as fast as they can to the bucket, holding on to the small ball or beanbag as they go.

Step 4: They will then stand up and put the object in the bucket.

Step 5: Next, they will roll back to the start.

Step 6: Repeat steps 1–5 until all the objects have made it into the bucket.

Make it a little easier: Don't use a potato sack or body sock. Simply have your child roll with their body.

Make it a little harder: Make it a race and time how quickly they can get the balls/beanbags in the bucket. Play with friends and see who can complete the task the fastest, or have two children race each other.

Baby Bonus Activity: Once your little one can walk, have them run or walk to carry the beanbags to the basket.

Additional Skills: Praxis

Upside-Down Puzzle

Description: This is a challenging activity that gets kids completing a puzzle in a whole new way. It works on building the muscles a child needs to sit in circle time at school. Note: This activity requires assistance from an adult throughout.

Materials:
- Jigsaw puzzle, Potato Head toy, or other buildable/multipart toy of your child's preference
- Small table (kid-size) or chair
- Yoga ball

Space: Small

Time: 10–15 minutes

Setup: Place the puzzle pieces behind the ball on the floor. Position a kid-size table or chair in front of the ball. Be sure that the surface of the table or chair can be reached at stomach level while the child is sitting on the ball. Put the frame of the puzzle on the table. The child will grab the pieces from the floor by reaching backward and then assemble the puzzle on the table.

Directions

Step 1: Have your child sit on top of the ball, while you support them at their knees or thighs. (Note: *An adult should support the child for the duration of the activity.*)

Step 2: Have your child slowly lean back so they are arching over the ball, like a backbend.

Step 3: They reach overhead and grab one piece of the puzzle.

Step 4: Return to sitting upright on top of the ball. (Encourage your child to get up without using their arms to push them up, like a sit-up. This movement will make those tummy muscles strong.)

Step 5: Once upright, your child places the puzzle piece where it belongs.

Step 6: Repeat steps 1–5 until the puzzle is complete.

Make it a little easier: Have the child lie on the ball on their tummy (instead of sitting on the ball and leaning over backward) to grab the pieces. They can then stand up and turn around to complete the puzzle.

Make it a little harder: When they're leaning backward over the ball, have them cross their hands over their chest when sitting up to make it more of a core strength exercise.

Baby Bonus Activity: Hold your baby on the ball and bounce them up and down (supporting them posturally). Lay them on their tummy on the ball and gently rock back and forth.

Additional Skills: Visual, Fine Motor

Backward Bowling

| 1 | 2+3 | 4+5 |

Description: Kids use their ingenuity to build a tower—then roll a ball at full speed toward the tower to send it tumbling.

Materials:
- Large blocks, bowling pins, or another buildable/stackable toy of your child's preference
- Small ball that is heavy enough to knock over the objects
- Balance board (optional)

Space: Small

Time: 5–10 minutes

Setup: Place a pile of blocks or other large stackable items on one side of the room and get ready to start building.

Directions

Step 1: Have your child stack the blocks to build a tower.

Step 2: Then, position your child to stand about five to ten feet in front of the tower with their back to it.

Step 3: Have them pick up the ball.

Step 4: Standing with legs wide, beyond shoulder's width, have them bend down at the waist, keeping their knees straight.

Step 5: They throw or roll the ball between their legs at the tower and send it tumbling.

Step 6: Repeat steps 1–5 until the entire tower is knocked down—then build it again.

Make it a little easier: Stand one to two feet in front of the tower instead of five to ten feet.

Make it a little harder: Have your child stand on a balance board while they construct the tower, working on both balance and core muscle strength as they build.

Baby Bonus Activity: An older sibling can build a tower and then let the baby topple it over, either with a parent holding the baby and swinging their feet into it, or letting the baby crawl or walk over to knock it all down. The baby might also be able to roll a ball to scatter the blocks.

Additional Skills: Praxis

Scooter Board Hockey

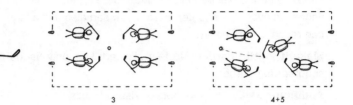

1+2   3   4+5

Description: No ice rink? No problem! Replace ice skates with scooter boards and get ready for the game.

Materials:
- Scooter board (one per child)
- Four cones or something that you can use to establish a boundary for a goal (two per goal)
- Handheld indoor hockey sticks, or pool noodles cut to size
- Small ball or indoor hockey puck

Space: Medium to large

Time: 20–25 minutes

Setup: Place two cones about five feet apart on opposite sides of the room or space, creating goals that are across from each other. Designate what is out of bounds so kids keep to the playing area.

Directions

Step 1: Separate the kids into teams and assign them a goal. One-on-one or two-on-two is best. This can also be done solo.

Step 2: Each child lies on their tummy on the scooter board in the middle of the playing area (equal distance between the goals) with the teams facing each other. Each child should have a hockey stick.

Step 3: Place a ball or hockey puck in the middle of the two teams, move out of the way, and say, "GO!"

Step 4: While prone (on their tummy) on the scooter boards, each child propels themselves forward using hands and feet, and then uses their stick to try to hit the ball into the other team's goal. (Remind them that sticks are for hitting only the ball or puck.)

Step 5: Once a team has scored, bring them back to the middle and start again.

Step 6: Have the kids play for a specific amount of time or until one team reaches a certain number of goals.

Make it a little easier: Ditch the hockey sticks and have the kids use their hands to hit the ball (remind the kids to be careful; it hurts to have a little finger run over by a scooter board). You can also use a larger ball so they can reach it more easily.

Make it a little harder: No feet allowed! Use only hands to propel the scooter board around.

Additional Skills: Proprioceptive, Visual, Praxis

Scooter Board BLASTOFF!

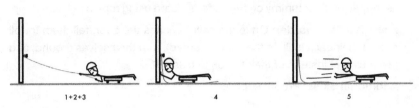

Description: This activity is a BLAST, and a scooter board is an excellent way to get vestibular input without using a swing.

Materials:
- Sturdy rope—about ten feet
- Scooter board
- Helmet
- Hula-Hoop (optional)

Space: Large

Time: 5–10 minutes

Setup: Tie a rope to a door (or sturdy surface) so that the child is pulling in the direction that it closes. Make sure the child's helmet is on.

Directions

Step 1: With their helmet on, the child lies on their tummy on the scooter board while facing the door. They are as far from the door as the length of the rope.

Step 2: Hand them the end of the rope and tell them to hold on with both hands.

Step 3: They pull themselves all the way to the door using the rope.

Step 4: Once they reach the door, they should put both hands against the door.

Step 5: Time to BLAST OFF! They should push hard against the door, propelling themselves backward.

Step 6: Repeat steps 1–5.

Make it a little easier: Instead of tying the rope to the door, pull your child as they lie on their tummy on the scooter board using rope or a Hula-Hoop.

Make it a little harder: Once the child reaches the door, tell them to roll over to their back (still on the scooter board), turn themselves around, and use their feet instead of their hands to blast off.

Additional Skills: Proprioceptive

Spin & Shoot

Description: An office chair is an easy way to get intense vestibular input without a swing. Spin & Shoot can provide powerful input, so watch your child's cues, make sure to take frequent breaks, and check in with your little one about how they feel.

Remember the following:
- The effects of vestibular input can have a delayed effect; so, take it slowly at first.
- It is important to always spin your child in both directions, so they get equal input from both ear canals.
- Choosing a proprioceptive activity (see pages 61) after this activity may be beneficial to help your child regulate.

Materials:
- Sturdy office chair on wheels (spinning office chair)
- Bucket
- Ball

Space: Medium

Time: 5–10 minutes

Setup: Put a large bucket about three to four feet away from the office chair. Place the office chair in an open area with nothing in range of being knocked over or run into.

Directions

Step 1: Have your child sit in the office chair.
Step 2: The child holds the ball in their lap.
Step 3: An adult spins the chair clockwise—not very fast.
Step 4: The child attempts to throw the ball into the bucket while the chair is spinning.
Step 5: Repeat steps 1–4, this time going counterclockwise.

Make it a little easier: Instead of your child trying to throw the ball while spinning, you spin the chair ten times, slowly and steadily, then stop the chair, and your child tries to throw the ball into the bucket. Be sure they also spin in the reverse direction (after a break to make sure they are not dizzy).

Make it a little harder: While your child spins in the chair, you hold the bucket and walk around, creating a moving target.

Baby Bonus Activity: Hold the baby in your lap while you sit in the swivel chair. Slowly spin clockwise five times, then five times counterclockwise.

Additional Skills: Visual

Infinity and Beyond

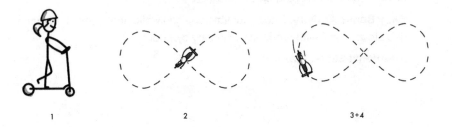

1   2   3+4

Description: To infinity and beyond (just like Buzz)! This activity is not actually *Toy Story* inspired, but you can tell your kids it is—and it's fantastic for their development.

Materials:
- Tape or chalk
- Bike, scooter, or scooter board
- Helmet

Space: Large

Time: 15–20 minutes

Setup: Draw a large infinity symbol (∞) with chalk on your driveway or use masking tape or painters' tape on the floor in a large open area of your house.

Directions

Step 1: Have your child put on their helmet and get ready.

Step 2: Have them move to the middle of the infinity symbol with whatever they choose to use—bike, scooter, or scooter board.

Step 3: They bike, scooter, or scooter board around the infinity symbol without losing balance or going off the line.

Step 4: Have them repeat steps 1–3 as many times as they can.

Make it a little easier: Instead of riding a bike around the infinity symbol, have your child walk around it.

Make it a little harder: Have your child walk backward around the infinity symbol without stepping off the line.

Baby Bonus Activity: Once your little one can walk, gently hold their hand and slowly stroll with them on the infinity symbol.

Additional Skills: Praxis

Indoor Broom Skating

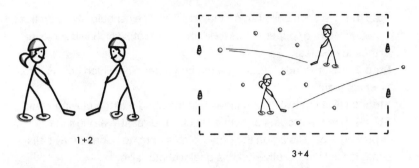

1+2

3+4

Description: This activity is a great way to offer a challenging activity while being stuck indoors on a rainy day.

Materials:
- Eight to ten small balls
- Four cones or other items to make two goals
- Child-size brooms or hockey sticks (one for each child)
- Helmets
- Coffee filters or paper plates (two for each child)
- Shaving cream or Mr. Bubble Foam Soap (optional)

Space: Large

Time: 35–40 minutes

Setup: Give each child either a paper plate or a coffee filter for each foot. Set up two goals on opposite sides of the room. Drop eight to ten balls in the middle of the playing area. This activity is good for one-on-one play but can be done solo as well (have your child shoot all the balls into one goal).

Optional: Spray the playing area with shaving cream for extra-slippery fun. Be careful! It gets more slippery than you might expect. (Spot-check before spraying to be sure that the shaving cream won't damage the floor.)

Directions

. . . .

Step 1: Have each child put on their helmet. They should stand on the coffee filters or paper plates (one for each foot), which will serve as their ice skates.

Step 2: Split the kids into two teams and determine which goal is for which team.

Step 3: Have the two teams face off in the middle of the playing area.

Step 4: Use the brooms or hockey sticks and "skate" around the playing area, sliding on the paper plates to try to get as many balls as possible in the other team's goal without falling.

Step 5: Repeat steps 1–4 as many times as the kids want to play.

Make it a little easier: Instead of using a broom or hockey stick to move the balls, the kids use their feet.

Make it a little harder: Use only one ball and make it more of a traditional hockey game.

Baby Bonus Activity: Spray shaving cream on the floor (or mat or disposable tablecloth) and let your baby crawl through it (making sure none gets in their mouth).

Additional Skills: Proprioceptive, Praxis

DIY Balance Board Ringtoss

1+2   3

Description: Balance can be a tricky skill, and balance boards are a fantastic way to work on it, but you don't need a fancy store-bought one. They are easy to make with materials from around your house.

Materials:
- Large couch cushion (or two)
- Standing paper towel holder
- Rings (large enough to fit over the paper towel holder), or you can cut out the center of paper plates to make a homemade version

Space: Small
- This can be done in a small place, but be sure to clear the area of any objects that could injure your child if they fall.

Time: 10–15 minutes

Setup: Place the cushion on the ground. You can stack two cushions to make it trickier to balance. Place the paper towel holder two to four feet in front of the cushions.

Directions

Step 1: Have your child stand on the cushion.
Step 2: Tell them to try to balance without falling or touching the ground.
Step 3: Now, while balancing, have them throw the rings, trying to get them to land on the paper towel stand (like a ringtoss game).
Step 4: Repeat steps 1–3.

Make it a little easier: Have your child hold on to a steady surface, such as a wall, while balancing.

Make it a little harder: Place the rings on the floor and have your child bend down to pick them up while on the cushions without losing balance. Then, toss them.

Baby Bonus Activity: Ditch the balance board and have your little one place the rings on the paper towel holder. Eventually, they can crawl over the balance board or couch cushion to get to the ring holder.

Additional Skills: Visual

Silly Swinging

Description: This activity is ideal for when you're outside at the park or at home on a swing set. Swings are an amazing way to provide children with vestibular input, and there are many ways to use them. Think outside the box.

Materials:
- Swing on playground or backyard swing set
- Ball or beanbag and target (optional)

Space: Yard or playground

Time: 15–20 minutes

Setup: As long as you have a swing available, no setup is necessary.

Directions

Step 1: Tell your child to lie on their tummy on the swing. Have them run forward, and once they have gone as far as the swing will let them, tell them to lift their feet. Encourage them to fly while riding back and forth on their tummy, keeping their feet up.

Step 2: Have them sit on the swing and spin it as fast as they can (the chains might twist up, and that is OK; they just need to stay on to unspin it). Make sure they spin in the other direction, too.

Step 3: They stand on the swing and balance while riding it back and forth.

Step 4: Next, they put one leg on either side of the swing and ride it like a horse.

Make it a little easier: The child sits on the swing and you push. Classic.

Make it a little harder: Try to throw a ball or beanbag at a target while on the swing. The target can be a parent who will catch the item.

Baby Bonus Activity: Gently swing the baby in an appropriate-size playground baby swing. Or an adult can hold a child in a football hold and rock them from side to side.

Additional Skills: Proprioceptive, Praxis

Beach Ball Bat

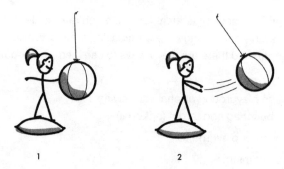

1   2

Description: Who says beach balls are only for the summer? Use them year-round with this activity.

Materials:
- Beach ball with string attached (or balloon)
- Couch cushion

Space: Large open space

Time: 5 minutes

Setup: Hang the beach ball from the ceiling or a doorway, or if you are outside, from a tree branch. Place the couch cushion—or stack two for more of a challenge—on the ground about six inches from the hanging beach ball.

Directions

Step 1: Have your little one stand on the cushion.

Step 2: Ask your child to hit the ball back and forth while balancing.

Make it a little easier: Don't use the cushions. Have them stand on the floor or ground.

Make it a little harder: Have them say the ABCs or sing another song while hitting the ball back and forth.

Baby Bonus Activity: Hang the ball close to the floor and have your baby hit the ball back and forth while seated.

Additional Skills: Visual, Proprioceptive

Silly Sliding

Description: Some people say that there is only one way to go down a slide, but the truth is, there are many.

Materials:
- Slide at playground or on backyard swing set

Space: Yard or playground

Time: 5 minutes

Setup: As long as you have a slide available, no setup is necessary.

Directions

Step 1: Tell your child to climb to the top of the slide.

Step 2: Have your child lie on their back with their head going down first.

Step 3: They slide down the slide on their back, upside-down. Wait at the bottom so you can catch them.

Make it a little easier: They sit on the slide and go down on their bottom.

Make it a little harder: They go down (safely) with their eyes closed.

Baby Bonus Activity: Place the baby in your lap and go down the slide together.

Additional Skills: Praxis

Additional Vestibular Activities

Think big movement to get your child active, and have fun while doing it. The best way is to head to the park—no bells or whistles needed.

Backyard/outdoor games
- Bike riding
- Bouncing on a yoga ball
- Gymnastics
- Ice skating
- Roller coasters
- Scootering
- Swings
- Trampoline

Board and other games
- Bilibo
- Sit 'n Spin
- Wooden balance board

3

INCREASING BODY AWARENESS

Enhancing the Proprioceptive Sense

. . . .

As I've mentioned, proprioceptive activities are a useful tool to follow the big, fast movements that engage the vestibular sense. After intense vestibular input increases the arousal level (leading to rambunctious behavior in some kids), the proprioceptive system helps to organize our little ones and calm their bodies in time for bed, school, or a trip to the grocery store. If the vestibular system is all about movement and our relationship with gravity, proprioception is about body awareness and our understanding of how we relate to our surroundings.

The proprioceptive system impacts coordination, body awareness, and force modulation (using the just-right amount of force, not too much or too little when throwing a ball, hugging, or giving a high five). The proprioceptive system works closely with the vestibular system for maintaining posture control and balance. All children need a healthy proprioceptive sense to navigate their environments. It enables them to run through a playground without bumping into the equipment or other children, gives them the ability to adjust their throw when playing baseball, and is even engaged when they get dressed in the morning.

Proprioception is one of my personal favorite senses. It has a powerful ability to ease us into relaxation. Proprioceptive input (which we often describe to parents as heavy work, like pushing and pulling or any action that is a force against your muscles) essentially helps us to stay grounded when we become overstimulated. It's like giving yourself a great big hug to regain control over a situation—literally, because giving someone a squeeze is proprioceptive input. I use it regularly. One night during the coronavirus pandemic, when I found myself awake at 4:00 a.m., I decided to take some of my own advice and turn to deep pressure (which is grounding but not technically proprioceptive input— but I won't get into the nitty-gritty here). I gathered every heavy blanket in my house, carried them to my bed, and stacked them on top of me. After a few turns from side to side, I finally fell asleep. The next morning, I bought a weighted blanket, which are everywhere now but just a few years ago could be found only in specialized sensory shops. I use it every night and for the first time since childhood, when I would ask my mom to tuck me in as tight as she could, have finally found a tool to help me sleep. My only question is why I suggested this to kids for years before I did it for myself.

My story is not unique. Kids who have trouble calming down often find proprioceptive activities to be their saving grace. A baby who sucks on their pacifier is using proprioception to regulate. This is the same reason that so many of us, like myself, chew on the ends of our pencils or bite our lips when we need to focus (like as I write this book). Recently, we got an email from a parent thanking us for helping her son understand his self-regulation and big tantrums. He independently began using his proprioceptive tools—rolling a weighted ball on his legs and spending time in his calming corner—and both he and his family were beyond proud when he was able to cool down before a massive eruption that would have ruined the day's plans.

CALMING TOOLBOX

We keep these tools handy to help our kids get heavy work throughout the day, and they're great to send to school with a child who is extra wiggly. I would love to see them in every classroom, in fact, because every kid needs a little help every once in a while to calm down and stay focused. (Note that we teach children that if one of these tools has become a toy, then it is no longer helping them regulate and it is time to try another. We'll say, "I can see your tool isn't helping your body right now—what do you think about switching it for a tool that might work better to help your body?")

- **Weighted ball to sit in their lap or roll on their legs**
  I choose a soft Pilates ball and not a weighted stuffy because a ball seems like less of a toy, whereas the stuffy can be distracting in a classroom.
- **Theraputty to squeeze and pull**
- **Squish ball**
  I like the ones that you can pull and stretch.
- **Exercise band**
  We teach kids to wrap it around the legs of their chair to play with at their feet. Or, if they are sitting on the ground, to put the band around their feet and behind their back with knees bent, and then their feet push against it.
- **Stretchy String Fidget (Monkey Noodle)**
- **Chew toppers for the pencil**
- **Chewelry necklaces**
- **Tangle BrainTools**
- **Hair clip**
  This is my personal go-to for every meeting, where you can find me clipping my fingers in my lap, and it's perfect for older children.

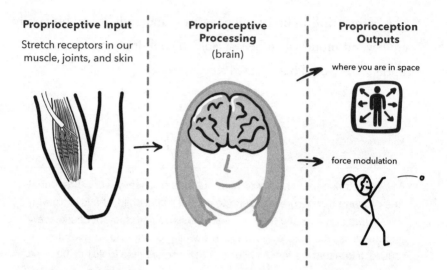

Proprioceptive Input

Stretch receptors in our
muscle, joints, and skin

**Proprioceptive
Processing**
(brain)

**Proprioception
Outputs**

where you are in space

force modulation

The Proprioceptive System

How the Proprioceptive System Works

Inside our muscles, skin, and joints we have special receptors that
sense when we move. They are activated by pressure on the skin or
when a muscle is stretched, which sends a signal to the nervous system, where a response is generated. When your little one gives you a
high five, their muscles are stretched as they move their arm, activating their proprioceptive sense to help them know where their hand is
in the air and guide it to move to connect with your hand (or miss
your hand). This is why we often refer to proprioceptive input as heavy
work; it is a load against the muscle, just like lifting weights for adults.
For kids, this could be climbing, yoga, or carrying heavy books or
other objects.

The proprioceptive system is responsible for helping your child be
aware of where their body is in their environment and to safely motor

plan, which means determining a path of movement and navigating a space. When your child is crossing the playground to say hi to their friend, they need to plan the best and safest path to get there without running into a moving swing or another child, and if they come across a broken piece of sidewalk or they feel a rock under their feet, their muscles adjust to account for the change in terrain. The proprioceptive system allows them to make changes to how they walk so they won't fall or lose their balance.

Have you ever heard the saying that someone is "like a bull in a china shop"? This characterization could apply to Tyler, who we met in the introduction. He is not only always on the move and bouncing off furniture and siblings alike, but he also tends to be a bit clumsy and has trouble picking up most sports. When someone struggles like this, it is often because they do not have a good sense of where their body is in space—a function of the proprioceptive system.

Children who have a well-developed proprioceptive sense will have confidence in themselves because they will be coordinated and able to move fluidly, with more ease, which makes it effortless for them to jump right into play. When I think of proprioception, I often think of athletes because they have an amazing sense of where they are in their surroundings (they are not stubbing their toes every day like I do) and because of that sense, they tend to be confident and join activities without hesitation, even if they've never played before.

If you put Tom Brady and me in a room and asked us to get through obstacles as fast as we could (perhaps a child's playroom after a rainy day, i.e., an explosion of LEGO pieces), chances are I would end up with a stubbed toe and a few bruises on my feet, while Tom would navigate that room without ever touching a stray LEGO brick. By virtue of his athletic abilities alone, I know that he is far more coordinated than the rest of us and has a better sense of where his body is in relation to things around him; in other words, his proprioceptive sense is functioning as well as any anyone's could.

Our proprioceptive system also allows us to use the appropriate amount of force to move our bodies or touch objects, as well as know the position of our bodies without using our eyes so that we can bring a favorite treat to our mouth or climb down a play structure. While the following may sound like "just" a game, we use it to measure the functioning of the proprioceptive system: Can you shut your eyes and still touch your nose with your forefinger? Can your child? You should be able to touch precisely the tip of your nose with your eyes closed.

A child who does not have a well-developed proprioceptive sense may be clumsy and have a hard time on the playground or even walking around their home or classroom without bumping into or breaking things. They may hold an egg so tightly that it breaks, overstuff their mouth with food, not put enough force into kicking a ball so it doesn't reach its target, or be unable to figure out how to climb a rock wall or karate chop. They may be unaware of how close they are to other objects and accidently bump into a table, spilling everyone's drinks, leading to teasing or social exclusion. It can be extremely frustrating for kids to constantly struggle to pick up a new skill, and because of this, they may become upset during challenging tasks or refuse to try new things that require body awareness. Some kids who struggle with proprioception may be labeled as being too rough. All of this can have a negative social and educational impact.

In a classroom, the proprioceptive sense supports a child's ability to write, cut, navigate the class, and perform fine motor skills. For example, in Josephina's classroom, they are making self-portraits for parent visiting day. Josephina needs to understand where her own body parts are located (e.g., her arms coming out of her body) so that she can draw a picture that resembles herself. It is also important for her to be able to walk through the classroom without bumping into the desks to hang her work of art on the wall and be ready for parent night.

The proprioceptive sense is essential for:

Body awareness: When we have a good sense of our body, we have a good understanding of spatial awareness. Body awareness impacts more than you might expect. For example, to have a proper grip on a pencil while writing, you need to be aware of your fingers without using your vision.

Force of movement: This allows a child to understand the right amount of force to use when doing everything from giving a high five to throwing a ball—especially if they're throwing that ball in the house or writing with a crayon that could break easily.

Self-regulation: We have talked a lot about how proprioception can have an extraordinary ability to help a little one balance themselves out, but when some children use proprioception to calm themselves, it can appear aggressive. I know that seems like an oxymoron, but it's true. A child may bite or squeeze their friends or family members because it provides them with proprioceptive input and helps them to calm or focus. Unfortunately, the same tool they use to regulate leads those friends to go running and brings trouble with their teacher or parent.

The proprioceptive system's organizing power can aid a child to increase their attention during school or in any situation where they need to stay calm. I suggest adding some proprioceptive activities to your household's daily routine; they're advantageous for all of us, especially before bed or after a big event filled with excitement and sugar, like a holiday or birthday party.

Motor planning and coordination: Because proprioception supports body awareness, spatial awareness, force modulation, and timing of movement, it has a massive impact on motor planning and coordination. If we see a child struggling with proprioception, we often see an impact on coordination as well.

Key Aspects of Proprioceptive Sense

Proprioceptive discrimination: A child who has a hard time distinguishing proprioceptive input will struggle to play tag or hand-clapping games. They may unintentionally slam doors or hug a bit tighter than they mean to, because they do not feel the difference in their body between using a lot of force or just a little. They may find it impossible to climb down a ladder without watching each foot on the rungs because they don't have the body awareness to feel where their foot is in relation to the ladder.

Proprioceptive modulation: Some children need heavy work to get a sense of where they are in relation to things around them. This is because they are under-responsive to proprioceptive input or need more input to understand where their body is in space. They might seem clumsier than other kids or have trouble keeping up on the playground. A child who struggles with proprioceptive modulation may also love rough-and-tumble play, or bite, push, walk on tiptoes, or hug and squeeze excessively, which can come across as aggressive and get them into trouble.

Proprioceptive Activities

. . . .

Laundry Relay

Description: I suggest this game after a birthday party or another exciting activity when your little one is having trouble settling down before bed. (Bonus: It helps parents get chores done.)

Materials:
- Two laundry baskets
- Clothes (or other soft objects)
- Timer

Space: Medium

Time: 5–15 minutes

Setup: Place a large pile of clothes (or dolls, dinosaur toys, etc.) on one side of the room and a second basket on the other side of the room. Feel free to have your child take the clothes from the dirty clothes hamper and use the washer as the second "basket" if you need to get some laundry done. It is the pushing of the weight that allows your little one to calm down.

Directions
. . . .

Step 1: Place an empty basket next to the pile of clothing.

Step 2: Set up a course for your child to follow using whatever objects you have on hand to be navigated around.

Step 3: Tell your child that you are going to have a relay race either against them (break out the laundry baskets!) or against the clock.

Step 4: When you start the clock, have your child put the pile of clothing into the basket.

Step 5: They then push the basket around some obstacles (the couch, kitchen island, toys on the floor, etc.) as fast as they can to reach the destination.

Step 6: They transfer all the clothes into the second basket. Then it's back to the start.

Step 7: Repeat steps 1–6.

Make it a little easier: Place lighter items in the basket, such as stuffed animals, and remove any obstacles in the way.

Make it a little harder: Instead of laundry, use weighted balls and add more twists and turns your child will have to take while avoiding the obstacles.

Baby Bonus Activity: As soon as your little one starts walking, you can have them carry items between baskets—just pick one at a time and offer lighter items. If your child is cruising and uses a walking toy, pushing on carpet also counts as heavy work.

Additional Skills: Praxis

Hot Diggity Dog

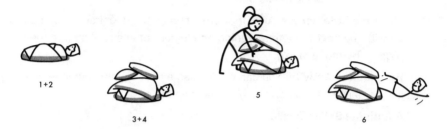

1 + 2

3 + 4

5

6

Description: This game not only supports the parent-child connection, it will also help your kid get calm and a sense of their body in space.

Materials:
- Blankets, bath towels, or beach towels
- Pillows

Space: Small
- Cuddle up in bed or on a couch.

Time: 5–15 minutes

Setup: All you need are a few nearby blankets and pillows.

Directions

Step 1: Get goofy and tell your little one that they look like a human hot dog.

Step 2: Tell them you need to get that hot dog in a bun. Have your child lie down on the blanket and wrap them up, like a big swaddle.

Step 3: Next, it's time for toppings! Ask your child what sort of toppings they want: Relish? Ketchup?

Step 4: With every topping, add another blanket or pillow (never covering their face).

Step 5: Give even squeezes down their body while you add each topping.

Step 6: Say, "Oh no! The hot dog needs to get free," and ask your child to wiggle out of the swaddle.

Make it a little easier: Place blankets over your child's body like they're a bit chilly, but don't swaddle them.

Make it a little harder: After they are a human hot dog, have them come up with the next food item, adding an element of imagination (are they a pizza, a burrito, a taco?).

Baby Bonus Activity: You can do this same activity with your little one—just be gentle. Use a baby blanket and skip the pillows!

Additional Skills: Tactile

Leap Frog

Description: This activity was inspired by one of my favorite games growing up, *Frogger*. It not only provides your child with proprioceptive input, but it will also get them belly laughing until they are exhausted.

Materials:
- Soft balls

Space: Large

Time: 10–15 minutes

Setup: All you need is a basket of balls.

Directions

Step 1: Have your little one get into a frog position—crouching with their knees bent and hands on the ground—on one end of the yard.

Step 2: Stand on the other side of the yard with the bucket of balls.

Step 3: Roll the balls in the general direction of your kids.

Step 4: Have your little ones hop to the other side of the yard without touching any of the rolling balls. Encourage them to take big leaps, coming all the way down to the ground (squatting with their hands between their legs) and then all the way up, like a star, with their feet off the ground.

Make it a little easier: Roll just one ball at a time.

Make it a little harder: Can your little one crab walk across the yard without touching any of the balls?

Baby Bonus Activity: Play a game of rolling the ball back and forth, or try to tag your little one with the ball and make them crawl, walk, or run away as fast as they can. When you catch them, give them lots of hugs, kisses, and love.

Additional Skills: Visual, Vestibular, Praxis

Bubble Pop

1   2   3

Description: Kids love Bubble Wrap—and it's always a plus to recycle!—and there are so many possibilities for turning it into a game.

Materials:
- Yoga ball
- Bubble Wrap

Space: Medium

Time: 5–15 minutes

Setup: A yoga ball with Bubble Wrap placed in front of it.

Directions

Step 1: Have your child lie on their tummy on the yoga ball, with their hands placed on the floor.
Step 2: Have them "walk" on their hands to the Bubble Wrap.
Step 3: They use their hands to pop the Bubble Wrap while balancing on the ball.
Step 4: Repeat steps 1–3 until all the Bubble Wrap is popped.

Make it a little easier: Pop the Bubble Wrap by jumping on it.

Make it a little harder: Move the Bubble Wrap farther from the ball so your child has to balance and use more strength.

Baby Bonus Activity: Forget the ball. Have them stomp away on that Bubble Wrap when they are crawling, walking, or—even better—when they start jumping.

Additional Skills: Tactile, Vestibular, Auditory

Bedbug Boogie

1+2   3   4

Description: Make sure those bedbugs climb out of your bed as quick as they can.

Materials:
- Bed with bedding

Space: Small

Time: 5–10 minutes

Setup: Tuck in the bedding on both sides of the bed, but leave the sheets and covers untucked with space at the head and foot, creating a little tunnel.

Directions

Step 1: Tell your little one that it's time to pretend to be bedbugs—and bedbugs love to boogie.

Step 2: Show your kid the hole at the foot of the bed and tell them the way to do the boogie is to wiggle through the hole as fast as they can to the other side.

Step 3: Have your child wiggle under the covers from the foot to the head of the bed as fast as they can.

Step 4: Repeat steps 1–3 to continue the boogie.

Make it a little easier: Don't tuck in the bedding at the sides of the bed.

Make it a little harder: Tuck in the bedding into the foot of the bed as well and have your little one pull it up to crawl under it.

Baby Bonus Activity: Instead of using the bed, take some cushions off the couch and let your little one climb on top of them.

Additional Skills: Praxis, Tactile

Shelter in Place

Description: This was one of my favorite snow day activities as a kid (or whenever I was trapped inside on any cold Midwest day). It is a lost art, but it is every child's right to destroy their living room in the process of building a fort.

Materials:
- Couch cushions
- Pillows
- Blankets

Space: Medium

Time: 30–45 minutes

Setup: No setup necessary; just pull the cushions off the couch and toss them in a pile.

Directions

Step 1: Have your child lean one couch pillow against the couch or another piece of furniture. This is one wall of their fort.

Step 2: They can then lean a second couch pillow against another object (like a coffee table).

Step 3: Time for them to place a third couch pillow on top, bridging the two.

Step 4: By placing a blanket over the three pillows, they now have a roof entrance to their fort.

Step 5: Let your child crawl inside to hang out in their gorgeous fort.

Make it a little easier: Set up all but one side of the fort and have your little one position the other wall.

Make it a little harder: Don't tell them how to set up the fort—let them use their imagination to design their own.

Additional Skills: Praxis

Water Loo

Description: An activity for a hot summer day in a bathing suit. This is also a wonderful way to help calm your little one's body after a trip to the ice cream shop.

Materials:
- Two large buckets or empty trash cans per child
- One beach pail per child

Space: Large

Time: 10–15 minutes

Setup: Fill one large bucket per child with water all the way to the top, and place it on one end of your yard. On the other end, place the other large empty bucket, one per child.

Directions

Step 1: Give each child a beach pail and have them stand next to a filled bucket.

Step 2: Instruct them to scoop water out of the filled bucket with their beach pail.

Step 3: Have them run across the yard as fast as they can and pour the water from the pail into the large empty bucket across the yard. Try not to spill!

Step 4: Once their pail is empty, they run back to the water-filled bucket and repeat as often as necessary.

Step 5: Whoever gets the most water from the first bucket to the second wins.

Make it a little easier: Move the two large buckets next to each other so they do not have to run with their pails.

Make it a little harder: Make it a race against the clock. Can they transfer all the water in under five minutes?

Baby Bonus Activity: Little ones love container play. Add a little water to a small bucket (or bowl), place an empty one next to it, give your baby a cup, and let them explore. Some water may get transferred, but chances are, most will end up on them or on the ground, and that is totally OK.

Additional Skills: Vestibular

Rock Formation

Description: I got this idea after a failed attempt at making rock candy during camp one summer. Instead, we made the recipe on a cookie sheet and chopped it into big pieces. Watching the kids use the hammer to break the candy into rocks, I realized that they were getting in some amazing heavy work.

Materials:
- Water
- Food coloring (I like to use an all-natural brand)
- Bowl
- Cookie sheet with a rim
- Rubber hammer

Space: Small

Time: 10–15 minutes

Setup: Mix water and food coloring in a bowl and pour it onto the baking sheet. Put it in the freezer until it is frozen solid.

Directions

Step 1: Place the cookie sheet with the colored ice on the table in front of your little one.

Step 2: Hand them a rubber hammer, reminding them to be careful and watch their fingers.

Step 3: Let them bang the giant sheet into small "rocks." You can pretend there is an earthquake or a giant stomping around.

Step 4: Put the rocks in the sink, turn on the water, and watch them melt away.

Make it a little easier: Only let the pieces partially freeze.

Make it a little harder: Draw spots on the ice or put a sticker in certain spots, and have your kid hit the spots and stickers.

Additional Skills: Auditory

Plunge 'n' Push

1+2   3   4

Description: Who knew a plunger could be used for something other than a clogged drain? Kids find this activity particularly hilarious.

Materials:
- A new or well-sanitized toilet plunger
- A scooter board

Space: Large

Time: 10–15 minutes

Setup: No setup necessary; just pick start and stop spots in the house.

Directions

Step 1: Have your little one sit on the scooter board.
Step 2: Tell them where the start and stop spots are.
Step 3: Give them the plunger to hold so they can propel themselves forward; you might have to demonstrate.
Step 4: Say go! See how fast they can get from the starting line to the finish line.

Make it a little easier: Forget the time and let them figure out how to use a tool (aka the plunger) to propel themselves forward.

Make it a little harder: Have them lie on their tummies on the scooter board and use the plunger to propel themselves forward.

Baby Bonus Activity: Once your little one can walk fluidly and has good postural control, sit them on the scooter board and let them use their legs to move around.

Additional Skills: Vestibular, Praxis

Clothing Shuffle

Description: How many times has your little one wanted to try on your clothes? Well, this is their chance.

Materials:
- A pile of your clothes, both tops and bottoms
- Timer (the one on your phone will do)

Space: Medium

Time: 10 minutes

Setup: Have a starting line and a finish line. At the starting line, place a pile of clothes, and at the finish line, a bell, or you can wait there to give out high fives.

Directions

Step 1: Place the pile of clothes at the starting line. If there is more than one child playing, set up a pile for each.

Step 2: Set a timer for five minutes.

Step 3: When you say "Go!" your kiddos have to put on as many of your clothes as they can, layering them on until the timer stops. If there are buttons, they've got to button them up; if there are zippers, they must zip.

Step 4: When the timer goes off, they need to run (or waddle) as fast as they can to the finish line.

Step 5: Whoever has the most pieces of clothing on wins.

Make it a little easier: Set the timer for ten or fifteen minutes instead of five.

Make it a little harder: When the kids run to the finish line, it's time to remove the clothes as fast as they can.

Additional Skills: Praxis, Tactile

At-Home Skiing

1   2   3

Description: Growing up, did you ever wear socks and slide around on the floors? This is a twist on that *Risky Business* move.

Materials:
- Large pillows
- Long rope
- Pillowcase, scooter board, blanket, or just socks

Space: Medium

Time: 5–10 minutes

Setup: Tightly tie the rope to the doorknob with the door shut, and make sure it cannot be opened even with your full weight. Put a pillow under the doorknob. Place the pillowcase at the other end of the rope.

Directions

Step 1: Have your little one stand on the pillowcase and hold the end of the rope.

Step 2: Tell them to begin pulling the rope, so they start to slowly slide across the floor toward the door.

Step 3: Have them keep pulling, ideally hand over hand, until they reach the pillow.

Make it a little easier: Hop toward the door in the pillowcase instead of pulling on the rope.

Make it a little harder: Say "Freeze!" a few times while they are pulling so they need to freeze and then start again.

Additional Skills: Vestibular

5 Little Monkeys

Description: This game goes along with the classic nursery rhyme. It may force you to break some rules, but that only makes it more enjoyable. I find parents sometimes get so caught up with rules that they've forgotten about old-fashioned entertainment like jumping on the bed.

Materials:
- Large couch cushions and mats
- Bed

Space: Small

Time: 5–10 minutes

Setup: Put mats and large couch cushions on the floor at the edge of the bed so it is safe for a child to jump off and crash into them. Make sure the entire perimeter is surrounded by pillows and there is nothing hard or sharp near the bed.

Directions

Step 1: Start to sing "Five Little Monkeys," and have your little one, well, jump on the bed.

Step 2: When you get to "one fell off and bumped his head," have your child jump off the bed into the crash pit you built with mats and pillows. Hold their hands to make it safer.

Step 3: As you sing "Momma called the doctor and the doctor said, 'No more monkeys jumping on the bed,'" get silly and give your little one a few squeezes on their body.

Step 4: Repeat steps 1–3, now saying four monkeys, three monkeys, two monkeys, one monkey. Continue until there are no more monkeys.

Make it a little easier: Your child drops to their knees on the bed instead of jumping onto the cushions.

Make it a little harder: When your little one crashes, they then have to pick a pose and freeze in that position for twenty seconds.

Baby Bonus Activity: Instead of using a bed and cushions, bounce your babe on your knees, and when it is time to fall, hold them while you separate your knees so they gently drop through your legs.

Additional Skills: Vestibular, Auditory

Mirror, Mirror

Description: This game requires your little one to use their proprioceptive sense to understand the position of their body.

Materials:
- Music
- Blindfold

Space: Small

Time: 10–15 minutes

Setup: Place the blindfold on your little one.

Directions

Step 1: Put your child's body in a funny position—it could be cactus arms, a star pose, etc.

Step 2: Start the music.

Step 3: Instruct them to dance, moving out of the position.

Step 4: When the music stops, they need to get their body back into the original position without taking the blindfold off.

Make it a little easier: Lose the blindfold.

Make it a little harder: Move more than their arms. Can you get them in a downward dog? Or twisted triangle?

Additional Skills: Auditory

Clowning Around

1   2   3

Description: This is another one that takes it back to childhood. Save it for a rainy day or play it outside.

Materials:
- Beanbags or small balls
- Large pillowcase

Space: Medium

Time: 10–15 minutes

Setup: Place the beanbags or balls around the floor (think Easter egg hunt).

Directions

Step 1: Have your kiddo step into the pillowcase like they're about to start a potato sack race.

Step 2: When you say "Go," they hop in the pillowcase to the beanbags around the room.

Step 3: They pick up a beanbag and place it into the pillowcase, without stepping out of the pillowcase themselves.

Step 4: Repeat steps 1–3 until they have picked up all the beanbags.

Make it a little easier: Hop without the pillowcase and collect the beanbags in a bucket.

Make it a little harder: Add a time limit and tell them to beat the clock. How fast can they go?!

Baby Bonus Activity: Put the beanbags around the room. Have your toddler pick them up and place them into a beach pail that they carry as they walk.

Additional Skills: Vestibular, Praxis

Fishie Find

Description: As a bonus for you, this one gets the beds stripped and ready for laundry.

Materials:
- Bedding or a pile of blankets/clothes
- Toy fish (or other toys)

Space: Small

Time: 5–10 minutes

Setup: Dump a big pile of blankets on the floor and hide toy fishies (or other toys) throughout.

Directions

Step 1: Tell your little one, "We need to find all the fishes and bring them back to their pond" (i.e., their storage container).
Step 2: Say "Go" and have them search through the blankets until they find a fish.
Step 3: Put the fish in the pond.
Step 4: Repeat steps 1–3 until all the fishies are found.

Make it a little easier: Put the fishies in visible spots on the blankets.

Make it a little harder: Hide the fishies under heavy pillows and in hard-to-find areas. You can even add a blindfold and make your child use their sense of touch to find them.

Baby Bonus Activity: Hide those fishies in a pile of light blankets on the floor and let your little one find them.

Additional Skills: Visual

Additional Proprioceptive Activities

Some of the best ways to develop the proprioceptive system don't require a structured game. Many are basic everyday tasks around the house. Bringing your kids in on these household activities will give them not only a sense of pride but also key proprioceptive input.

Backyard/outdoor games
- Carrying a backpack
- Gardening
- Pushing the cart at a grocery store
- Watering plants
- Digging in sand or dirt
- Climbing up a slide

Indoor chores and games
- Carrying groceries
- Doing laundry
- Moving chairs
- Putting books away
- Taking out the trash
- Vacuuming
- Wiping tables and windows
- Playing with clay
- Using squeeze toys
- Doing animal walks (walking around like their favorite animal)
- Doing wall pushes (you can suggest that the room feels smaller to you and enlist your child to help push the walls to try to make the room bigger)
- Jumping on the bed
- Rolling a weighted ball

4

GETTING IN TOUCH

Strengthening the Tactile Experience

. . . .

Now that you have learned about two of our "hidden" senses, let's take a look at a better-known one—the tactile system, otherwise known as our sense of touch. I have noticed that sensory play is most often associated with tactile play.

Have you ever heard of a sensory bin? You've probably seen examples on Pinterest of containers filled with uncooked rice or beans that conceal little toys. These days they're in every preschool classroom and many home playrooms. Most parents are familiar with a tactile bin—and particularly the mess it causes when it spills all over the floor—but they often don't know exactly why having their little ones stick their hands in these bins is important for their development. The truth is that the tactile system is fundamental in helping us accomplish daily tasks like tying shoes (a skill that children are learning at progressively later ages these days), writing, getting dressed, using utensils, eating a variety of foods, and many aspects of self-care.

Before we jump in, I want to tell you about a little girl who was creative and loved playing with her friends and exploring her environment, but if you tried to put her into a pair of jeans, you would see this generally content child turn into an unhappy banshee. Her clothes had to be soft stretch pants or dresses. Her peers often put stickers on their arms and pretended they were tattoos, but even the thought of a sticker on her skin made her feel sick. She also hated face paint and had to wash her hands the minute they got dirty. Growing up in the Midwest, where playing in mud puddles was common, she would often sit and watch because no way was mud getting anywhere near her. Eventually she hit middle school, where she gave in to wearing jeans to fit in, but the minute she was home, those pants were exchanged for something more comfortable. Flash-forward to adulthood, she ended up being an occupational therapist who specializes in sensory integration—and who still has a strong preference for dresses and leggings, stays away from face paint, and avoids the slime trend as much as she possibly can. You've probably guessed by now: that little girl is me. I have always struggled with textures, including certain foods. Things turned around during OT school, when I finally understood my own sensory system—I know to prepare myself if I will be working on the tactile system with a client and am able to tolerate a range of textures—but I'm still sensitive. A few weeks ago, when one of our therapists put foam all over a ball to play catch with a child and then threw me the ball without warning, I quickly jumped away in an instinctive avoidant response.

Our tactile system helps us distinguish between qualities of touch. It tells us about the pressure of touch (light versus deep), as well as pain, temperature, and qualities of textures. It helps our little ones to reach without looking into their toy box and pick up their doll's hairbrush, or into their desk to grab their pencil. We use it when we reach into our purse for keys or find an item in the diaper bag without turning on the light in the baby's room. The tactile sense is crucial for staying safe, too. It tells you if the bathwater is too hot or if a pointy stick is poking you during a picnic so you can adjust to avoid it. The tactile system can have an impact on our emotions, and we can communicate our emotions through touch—like offering a gentle back rub to signal that Mommy is here, it is OK.

The tactile system also works with the proprioceptive system to create what is called the somatosensory system, so we can understand the exact position of our bodies. It lets us feel that smear of chocolate on our face and get it off without looking in the mirror. It also is central to coordination. Kids who struggle with their somatosensory system tend to be a bit clumsier, messier, and more disorganized than their friends.

When children are extremely picky eaters, it often has to do with the texture, not just taste, of the food. We have one little guy, Cruz, at Play 2 Progress who came to us because eating any food that was not hard with a crunch caused him to gag. He could not tolerate soft textures, not even the universally adored mac 'n' cheese. We learned that going to the beach was not an option for Cruz because the sand was too much for him to handle, and despite wanting to participate in cooking activities at his preschool, he could not touch dough with his hands. His parents didn't mind his disdain for the beach (although it does put a crimp in living in LA) or that he didn't like getting messy, but he wasn't getting the nutrition he needed, and it wasn't sustainable for them to constantly freeze-dry fruits and veggies so Cruz could eat something hard and crunchy. It has been a long process, encouraging him to use his hands to explore various textures and giving him permission to try—and spit out—softer foods, but recently he has been able to eat pasta and other new meals (and just in the nick of time, too, as during the coronavirus pandemic, his parents had less access to his favored foods).

At Play 2 Progress, we have a tactile room where we encourage parents to allow their babies to get—and stay—messy. They should be exposed to a variety of textures while they are young, and if we constantly wipe their faces and hands, they don't get to experience the feeling of being a bit untidy, and learn that it's OK. Getting mussed up is a great way to get used to tactile sensations. If you come into one of our Parent & Me classes during a tactile activity, you will see babies in their diapers crawling over spiky balls and soft balls and through foam soap, and playing with veggie paint (see page 93).

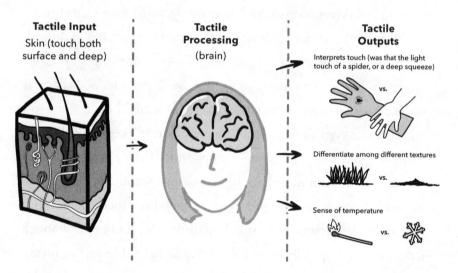

The Tactile System

How the Tactile System Works

Inside our skin, both on the surface and in the deeper layers, we have different types of receptors that are activated by tension on the skin, vibration, contact, temperature, and pressure. Some of these receptors are quick acting, and others respond slowly, allowing you to distinguish in more detail what you are touching—determining the difference between a dime and a penny in your pocket, for example. These sensations travel to multiple areas in the brain, where a response is generated. If you touch a hot pan, the response is going to be to quickly pull your hand away.

Touch is also tied to emotional state—which, if you haven't caught on to the theme by now, like all sensory input can impact our self-regulation and emotional state. You may have heard of the benefits of skin-to-skin contact for preemie babies and how it can promote their ability to thrive and bond. Skin-to-skin contact is now widely used in hospitals and birthing centers for both premature and full-term babies immediately after birth and throughout the fourth trimester. It's amazing for bonding, but that type of contact is also enormously soothing. You may already know how your touch can comfort an infant who is teething or suffering from an ear infection when they wake in the middle of the night.

The tactile system can work this way for all of us. You know after a hard day, when all you want is a friend or partner to give you a massage or pull you into a hug and make you feel a little bit better? That is the influence of the tactile system.

Beyond its comforting influence, touch can inspire a range of responses. While a gentle deep touch, like a hug, can slow our heartbeat and bring calm, an unexpected one can startle us and increase our heartbeat, creating upset or agitation. How many times have you jumped when something unexpectedly brushed the back of your arm? I am terrified of spiders, and the touch of a strand of hair or a leaf can send me into a full-on panic until I'm able to figure out what I'm feeling.

The tactile system is also responsible for something called tactile discrimination, which is the ability to differentiate among textures. This is what all those sensory bins holding hidden toys are for—helping them distinguish, by touch, among items. The ability to tactilely discriminate also allows your child to successfully undertake independent actions like buttoning a shirt or zipping a zipper. In order to tie their shoes, a child needs to be able to feel the laces in their fingers to successfully manipulate them into a tie. (Besides the sensory implications, a child still wearing Velcro shoes in fifth grade is at risk of being bullied.) An example that I often see with elementary school children is being able to tie back their hair into a ponytail, which is necessary for kids who have long hair and for when they play with Barbies and other dolls.

The tactile and proprioceptive systems work together to contribute to our overall handwriting and coordination—or lack thereof. In school, children need to be able to manipulate pencils, crayons, and paintbrushes. Handwriting in particular requires precise movement and the ability to control the pressure needed to hold a pencil firmly in a proper grip and keep it on the paper to write fluidly and legibly. Kids need to feel the crayon in their hand as it makes contact with the paper, so they don't press too hard and break the crayon or tear the sheet while coloring.

Have you ever felt a fly land on your arm and without looking immediately slapped it away, or have you been able to brush off the crumbs around your mouth without looking in the mirror? Can you imagine if you couldn't locate exactly where that fly or piece of croissant was, and you just knew something was wrong? Our ability to know where something is touching us and its qualities contributes to our overall coordination or clumsiness. If Andre brushes up against the Magna-Tile tower, he knows to move away slowly so he doesn't knock it over and upset his friends.

One of the most well-known symptoms of a sensory-processing challenge is tactile defensiveness—reacting negatively or out of proportion to a sensation that wouldn't bother most children. We see it all the time at work, and my own childhood experience fits this to a T. We encourage parents to recognize that if their little one is crying or lashing out, it's not because they are misbehaving but because they actually feel uncomfortable following tactile input, leading to distress. This can be extremely disruptive to daily life. When hair washing feels like pins and needles, a child will naturally try to avoid baths. To this day I cringe at the thought of my mom brushing my hair when I was little—it hurt. She wasn't being rough (at least I don't think she was); my sensory system was just firing in a way neither of us understood at the time.

Many kids who struggle with tactile defensiveness have a hard time finding comfortable clothes, showering or bathing, and playing with others—especially in crowded spaces. If they're bothered by their peers rubbing against them or the feeling of the sand in their socks, they may hang on the outskirts of the playground. They may avoid a kiss from their grandma or refuse to join in on family cuddles during movie night—everyone's little movements and different clothes is just too much tactile sensation. It is important to repeat this point: your children are not being stubborn; they are physically uncomfortable with the sensations they're interacting with. The seam on the sock really does bother them. No offense to Grandma, but even a gentle arm rub (especially if a scratchy sweater is involved) can feel overwhelming.

Sensory bins are an easy way to work on tactile defensiveness. From the time your baby is born, have them explore a range of textures. Move tummy time to the grass or a textured mat. Give them toys that are soft and fuzzy; hard and smooth. Let them play with their food and explore the soap in the bath. In the kitchen, encourage them to touch and explore all the ingredients for a meal before you cook them. As soon as they are ready to move beyond purees and eat solids, introduce a variety of foods so they can tolerate various textures and be more adventurous with taste as they get older. Let them eat with their hands. Don't reach for a wipe the minute they have a mess on their face or hands. Let them feel it and spend time with it before cleaning up or taking a bath. (One of my favorite sights is a diaper-clad baby on the beach covered in sand as they rub seaweed and water all over their tummy and hair.) You can even make safe-to-eat veggie and fruit paints (see page 93) and let them get sloppy. Safety note: Be sure to avoid choking hazards like hard raw vegetables and fruits, nuts, seeds, raisins, hard candy, grapes, popcorn, and hot dogs. Always keep an eye on your baby while they are eating—particularly if it is a new food item.

Some kids are less sensitive to touch and want lots of tactile input. This is the little one that you leave with the finger paints for one minute and come back to find a child covered head to toe in color. They are the first one to jump in the mud puddle, happily play with slime, and often have their faces covered with their lunch. Much like our clients who struggle with tactile defensiveness, those who love a ton of tactile input may have issues with modulating and integrating that input. Instead of over-responding, however, they under-respond, unable to sense how much mud is covering their body or the food that's been on their cheek for hours, or they may seek out tactile input.

Key Aspects of Tactile Sense

Tactile discrimination: This is the ability to properly process the various qualities of touch. It is why we can reach into a desk without looking and get a pencil and not the scissors. If a child struggles here, they may be unable to distinguish between textures. Remember Tyler, who bear-hugged his sister and friends with a bit too much force? He also may find it tough to pull something out of his toy box without using his eyes. Another child may not know that a Cheerio is stuck to their face until midafternoon, or they might have trouble getting dressed and tying their shoes.

Tactile modulation: Going back to "Goldilocks"—we need the just-right response. A kid may have a reaction that is bigger or smaller than what you would expect, or they may crave excessive tactile input—you find them splashing around naked in the mud after it rains or bothering their friend by repeatedly touching their soft sweater. Mikey is an example of a child who can't get enough tactile input. Every day at preschool he can be found with his shirt off or rubbing sand all over his body.

We've spent much of this chapter discussing tactile defensiveness, which is when a child is overly reactive to touch and texture. That sock may feel painful, or they don't like catching the spiky ball. This is not the child being "sensitive" or uncooperative—their nervous system is on alert, which makes a particular item feel disproportionately uncomfortable. I really can't say it enough: it is crucial that you understand that your child is having a legitimate reaction and that you don't force them to do anything that makes them uncomfortable. If they are in a constant state of fear that they will be touched or forced to wear clothes that irritate them, you can imagine how hard it will be for them to jump in at the playground or make slime with their friends. On the flip side, a child may seem to have a high pain tolerance because they are under-responsive to stimulation and don't detect the discomfort or the temperature of whatever they just touched, which has obviously dangerous implications.

Tactile Activities

Beaded Treasure

Description: This activity uses a tactile medium that I could spend hours playing with: water beads.

Materials:
- Water beads (or any textured item you have around the house, such as beans, pasta, or rice)
- Large container
- Pony beads or LEGO pieces
- Blindfold
- Pipe cleaner or string

Space: Small

Time: 10–15 minutes

Setup: Dump the water beads (or beans, pasta, or rice) into the large container. Mix in the pony beads.

Directions

Step 1: Blindfold your little one.

Step 2: Place their hands in the mix of water beads and pony beads (or LEGO pieces).

Step 3: Tell them to use their sense of touch and find as many pony beads (or LEGO pieces) as they can.

Step 4: Remove the blindfold.

Step 5: Thread the beads onto the pipe cleaner to make a bracelet or necklace. If using LEGO pieces, have your child connect them in a row or tower.

Make it a little easier: Instead of using pony beads, use a bigger toy such as TinkerToys or Magna-Tiles.

Make it a little harder: Instead of removing the blindfold before making a bracelet or necklace, keep it on and have your child use their sense of touch to get the beads on the pipe cleaner.

Additional Skills: Fine Motor

Shaving Cream Ice Skating

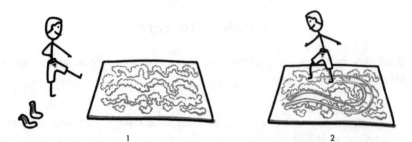

1   2

Description: This is a fan favorite at Play 2 Progress, and it's an easy way to expose kids to different textures.

Materials:
- Yoga mat, play mat, or Slip 'N Slide
- Shaving cream (we like Mr. Bubble Foam Soap)

Space: Large
- Choose a space that you won't mind getting a little dirty—this is a messy activity.

Time: 10–15 minutes

Setup: Put the mat on the ground and cover it with *tons* of shaving cream.

Directions

Step 1: Take off your little one's socks and roll up their pants. Or get everyone into bathing suits and call it ice skating at the beach.
Step 2: Your child pretends to be in a snowy landscape and starts skating—that is, slipping and sliding barefoot on the mat.
Step 3: Wipe off their feet with a towel and have them jump right in the bath (they'll need it).

Make it a little easier: Instead of ice skating, have your child slide on their belly in the foam by adding it to a slide or a play ramp.

Make it a little harder: Add a few obstacles for your child to avoid, like cones or a few pots on the ground.

Baby Bonus Activity: Let your baby crawl right through that foam.

Additional Skills: Vestibular, Proprioception

Veggie Finger Paint

Description: Finger paint is fun, but there is always the fear that our little ones will put the paint in their mouths. Our older kids love painting using their own creations and exploring the various colors they can make with foods. If you don't want to make your own veggie paint, you can use prepackaged purees.

Materials:
- Turmeric, berries, or any colorful vegetable (soft and cooked)
- Flour
- Water
- One bowl per paint color
- Potato masher
- Large spoon
- Blender (for hard-to-smash fruits/veggies)
- Paper

Space: Small
- A kids' table in the kitchen

Time: 20+ minutes

Setup: Chop the veggies and fruits into small pieces.

Directions

Step 1: Smash or blend your fruit and cooked veggies into a puree. Your little ones will love smashing the berries with their fingers, or you can blend them. I usually let the kids mash them first and then pop what remains in the blender.

Step 2: Mix water into the puree until you have a smooth and even mash. It may be runny or have some chunks in it, and that is OK. It does not need to be perfectly smooth.

Step 3: If you would like to thicken your paint a bit, add some flour slowly and stir until you have your desired thickness.

Step 4: Start painting! I suggest they use their hands, but a new paintbrush works, too.

Make it a little easier: Make the paint for your little one.

Make it a little harder: Let them come up with the fruits and veggies to use that will make colorful paint. Encourage them to experiment.

Baby Bonus Activity: Strip them down to their diaper, make the paint, get them on the floor, and let them go for it. Allow them to cover themselves in veggie paint; they may even try a few bites, which is OK as long as they are cleared for eating.

Additional Skills: Fine Motor

Nut Butter House

Description: How many times have you watched your child create master-pieces out of their Magna-Tiles or blocks? This activity uses that same creativity while engaging their tactile system.

Materials:
- Graham crackers
- Nut butters
- Bowl
- Plate

Space: Small

Time: 20+ minutes

Setup: Put the nut butter in a bowl and the crackers on a plate.

Directions

Step 1: Give your little one the supplies and tell them that they get to make a special structure or house out of crackers and nut butter.

Step 2: Let them use their hands to spread the nut butter as the glue on the edges of the crackers and stick them together to build a house.

Step 3: Repeat with new foods. Can they make a celery teepee?

Make it a little easier: If your child is having trouble touching the nut butter, let them use a firm paintbrush or small spoon.

Make it a little harder: You make a structure first and have them build one that looks the same.

Additional Skills: Fine Motor, Visual

Elephant Poo

Description: You've probably seen this recipe for oobleck before, and maybe you've even made it yourself. One day during Jungle Camp we decided to call it elephant poo, and the kids found it all the more hilarious and engaging. So, elephant poo it is.

Materials:
- Cornstarch
- Water
- Bowl
- Brown food coloring
- Measuring cup
- Plastic table covering or floor mat

Space: Small

Time: 20+ minutes

Setup: Place all the supplies on the table. Have your child wear clothes that you won't mind getting dirty. They can also wear a smock to protect their clothes from getting stained with food coloring.

Directions

Step 1: Add one part water and two parts cornstarch to a bowl. I suggest starting with one cup of water and two cups of cornstarch.

Step 2: Have your child use their hands to start mixing until everything is well combined.

Step 3: Add a few drops of food coloring (brown or green for the poo), and mix in with a spoon.

Step 4: They start exploring the change in texture the elephant poo takes from when it is in their hands to how it is in the bowl. Help them observe that it seems like a liquid in the bowl but changes to a solid in their hands.

Make it a little easier: Pre-make the elephant poo, and then let your child play with it.

Make it a little harder: Can your little ones determine which colors to mix to make brown food coloring?

Additional Skills: Proprioceptive

Blind Puzzle

1   2   3

Description: You don't have to work with messy materials to engage the tactile system. This is a no-mess activity that will still support your child's sense of touch.

Materials:
- One empty tissue box, square or rectangular
- Four toilet paper cardboard tubes that will fit in the tissue box; cut them to make them smaller if they don't fit
- Blindfold

Space: Small

Time: 5–10 minutes

Setup: Place the toilet paper tubes on one side of your little one and the tissue box on the other.

Directions

Step 1: Blindfold your little one.

Step 2: Have them feel around to find both the tubes and the box. I like making sure the hole in the tissue box is not facing up, so they need to feel and turn the box to find it.

Step 3: Ask them to put the tubes into the box using only their sense of touch.

Make it a little easier: Place the tissue box and each toilet paper roll in their hand so they don't need to feel to find them.

Make it a little harder: Add a timer.

Baby Bonus Activity: Forget the blindfold. Let them explore with container play.

Additional Skills: Fine Motor

Seek 'n' Grab

Description: This is one of my go-to activities to work on tactile discrimination. It will also pass the time on a long flight.

Materials:
- Empty bag that you cannot see through, like a small drawstring bag
- Small toys, cars, blocks, small action figures, or plastic animals
- Blindfold

Space: Small

Time: 10–15 minutes

Setup: Place the small toys inside the bag. Pay attention, because you'll need to remember what they are.

Directions

Step 1: Blindfold your child or, if you have a drawstring bag, they can use only their hand to reach in, without seeing what's inside.
Step 2: Tell them which item to grab.
Step 3: Only using their sense of touch, they grab the item you suggested.

Make it a little easier: Include only two or three items.

Make it a little harder: Choose items that feel the same but have a number of shapes, like tangrams.

Baby Bonus Activity: Put textured balls or toys in a bag and have your baby reach in to pick one out.

Additional Skills: Fine Motor

Messy Foot Spa

Description: You may have seen foot spas filled with water beads for kids, and those are pretty cool, but we know everything is a little more fun when it feels like you are at the beach.

Materials:
- Sand (you can also blend cereal to make homemade sand)
- Bucket, foot tub, or basin big enough for your little one to stick both feet inside
- Chair at a height so their feet touch the bottom of the bucket
- Water
- Food coloring (optional)
- Marbles (optional)

Space: Small

Time: 15–20 minutes

Setup: Place sand in the bottom of the bucket and add water until it is a little more than halfway filled. Add blue food coloring if you want it to look like the ocean.

Directions

Step 1: Put on some quiet music.
Step 2: Have your child put their feet in the bucket and explore how the sand feels on their feet.
Step 3: Add the marbles for an additional texture experience.
Step 4: Repeat with other textures. What if you put cornstarch in the bucket? Rice? Beans?

Make it a little easier: If your child struggles with the texture, let them wear water shoes or socks.

Make it a little harder: Can they find hidden marbles in the sand with their feet?

Baby Bonus Activity: Let them sit in the basin or tub.

Additional Skills: Proprioceptive

Pasta Art

Description: This will bring back camp memories of making spaghetti necklaces and suns out of dry pasta—with a colorful twist.

Materials:
- Finger paint (nontoxic)
- Bowls (one per color of paint)
- Plates (one per color of paint)
- Dried pasta (preferably short cylinders, like penne or rigatoni)
- Paper
- Glue
- String if you are making a necklace (optional)
- Smock

Space: Small

Time: 30+ minutes

Setup: Pour a good amount of each paint color into separate bowls. Have plates ready for each color as well. Put a covering on the table to protect from spills. Give your child a smock to wear to keep paint off their clothes.

Directions

Step 1: Pour some dry pasta into the individual bowls with the paint.

Step 2: Tell your child to use their hands to mix the pasta around, making sure it is fully coated. Tell them it is OK to make a mess.

Step 3: Scoop the pasta out of the bowls and put the pieces onto a plate to let them dry—one plate for each color. You may want to put some wax paper on the plate, so they don't stick.

Step 4: Once dry, place the pasta on a string to make a necklace or glue the colored pastas on paper to make a design. What will they come up with?

Make it a little easier: As always, if your little one struggles with texture, let them put on some gloves or let them mix the pasta and paint with a spoon.

Make it a little harder: Can they mix it blindfolded? Or can they mix paint with their hands to make more colors?

Baby Bonus Activity: Let them mix cooked pasta with their hands.

Additional Skills: Fine Motor

Rainbow Spaghetti Dinner

Description: Remember how exciting it was to eat green eggs and ham for a special occasion? What about rainbow spaghetti?

Materials:
- Cooked spaghetti
- Large bowl
- Small bowls
- Food coloring
- Ziploc bags

Space: Small

Time: 10–15 minutes

Setup: Once the pasta is cooked, allow it to cool before placing it in a big bowl. If you want multiple colors, separate the pasta into a few bowls.

Directions

Step 1: Be sure your child washes their hands really well.

Step 2: Place a few drops of food coloring into the bowl.

Step 3: Pour the cooked pasta into the bowl.

Step 3: Let your child mix the color into the pasta with their hands until it is uniform.

Step 4: Repeat the process for the other colors of your child's rainbow.

Step 5: Plate the rainbow spaghetti, add toppings, and enjoy.

Step 6 (optional): If you don't want to eat the pasta, rainbow pasta can also go into a sensory bin. Add it to a large container, and let your little one put their hands and feet in to explore the texture. They can also cut and rip the noodles.

Make it a little easier: Use a spoon to mix.

Make it a little harder: Have your child use two hands at once to mix.

Baby Bonus Activity: Get them into their diaper, lay down a tarp or towel outside, and let them put the pasta all over their body.

Additional Skills: Proprioceptive

Chalk Walk

| 1 | 2 | 3 |

Description: This exercise was inspired by one of my childhood favorites—making tracks in the snow! Now that I live in sunny Southern California, I adapted it to something our almost always barefoot kids could do.

Materials:
- Chalk

Space: Medium

Time: 5–10 minutes

Setup: No setup necessary. Just make sure you have an empty driveway or sidewalk, or do it at the playground.

Directions

Step 1: Rub a lot of chalk on the bottoms of your little one's feet and hands. I find it is helpful to break the chalk so it rubs easier on their feet.

Step 2: Have them create a path with their footprints and handprints for you to follow. They can even add a hopscotch or do a few yoga moves.

Step 3: Follow their path, or have a friend see if they can track them.

Make it a little easier: You mark out the path and have them follow it. Maybe make a hopscotch game for them to jump through.

Make it a little harder: Have them create an obstacle course using only their footprints. Can they hop? Jump on one foot?

Baby Bonus Activity: Rub their feet in chalk and let them walk around. Show them their footprints, or let them stamp them on paper.

Additional Skills: Praxis

Foam Art

Description: This is another popular one with our kiddos. It is a cool, textured variation on plain old finger painting.

Materials:
- Colored foam soap (we like Mr. Bubble)
- Glue
- Construction paper
- Bowl
- Tarp or old clothes (for protection from splatter or drips)

Space: Small

Time: 20–25 minutes

Setup: Place all the supplies on the table.

Directions

Step 1: Squirt about a cup of foam soap in the bowl.

Step 2: Pour about a cup of glue into the foam.

Step 3: Mix the glue and foam thoroughly with a spoon.

Step 4: Spread enough on the construction paper until the whole sheet is covered in a thin layer of the foam-and-glue mixture.

Step 5: Tell your child to use their pointer finger to create a picture or write their name in the foam soap.

Step 6: Let it dry and marvel at the art.

Make it a little easier: No need to make art from the foam. Hide toys inside the bowl and let your child explore the texture.

Make it a little harder: Can they write their name in the foam while blindfolded?

Additional Skills: Fine Motor

Abstract Ball Paint

Description: I am a big fan of children's abstract paintings, and I frame them for unique wall art. Decorate your walls with the gem your child will design.

Materials:
- Small balls (even better if you have a variety of textures and sizes)
- Paint (whatever color or colors your child likes)
- One container for each color of paint, big enough so balls can get covered, but not so big that balls will get lost in the paint
- Paper

Space: Medium

Time: 15–20 minutes

Setup: Pour one color of paint into each container. Protect the area and your child from spills and splashes.

Directions

Step 1: Have your child roll a ball in the paint, and make sure it is fully covered.
Step 2: They roll it all around the paper to create their abstract painting.
Step 3: Repeat steps 1–2 with more colors.
Step 4: Let the painting dry and tack it up.

Make it a little easier: Use gloves to roll around the paint-covered ball, or put the paper and ball on a tray and shake it to spread the paint.

Make it a little harder: Put the paper on the ground and gently push the ball around it. If you want to go big, your child can paint your driveway using a soccer ball and chalk paint.

Additional Skills: Visual

Car Wash

Description: This keeps kiddos occupied for hours in the kitchen or outside on a sunny day.

Materials:
- Liquid dish soap
- Water bins or large bowls
- Bucket of water
- Towel
- Toy cars (or other small toys)
- Scrub brush

Space: Medium

Time: 25+ minutes

Setup: Pour a good amount of dish soap into bowl, and add just a bit of water.

Directions

Step 1: The car wash is open! Have your child put the first car into the soap and use their hands and the scrub brush to scrub it clean.

Step 2: Now they can move the car to the water bucket and rinse it.

Step 3: Place the car onto the towel for drying.

Step 4: Repeat until all the cars are done.

Make it a little easier: Use only water.

Make it a little harder: Add a scrub brush to encourage bilateral coordination.

Additional Skills: Fine Motor

Citrus Stamps

Description: This is another way for your child to produce a beautiful picture fit for the fridge.

Materials:
- Citrus fruits
- Paper
- Water-based paint
- Plate
- Knife

Space: Small

Time: 25+ minutes

Setup: Pour some paint on a plate and slice the citrus fruits in half.

Directions

Step 1: Have your child dip the fruit into the paint, flesh side down.
Step 2: They push the fruit with paint onto the paper to make a stamp.
Step 3: Repeat with more colors.

Make it a little easier: Pre-dip the fruit.

Make it a little harder: Have them help you slice the fruit in half.

Additional Skills: Olfactory

Additional Tactile Activities

Tactile play can be messy. Remember to embrace the mess and resist the wipes.

Backyard/outdoor games
- Playing in the grass
- Playing in the mud
- Making sandcastles
- Stomping barefoot in puddles

Board and other games
- Finger paints
- Play-Doh
- Clay
- Rice bins
- Sandbox/sand table
- Bean bins
- Water beads
- Cooking using the hands (not utensils)
- Stickers
- Exploring materials with different textures
- Feel & Find game
- Tactile Search and Match game

5

SEEING CLEARLY

Honing the Visual System

. . . .

Let's dive into the very sense you are using right now—vision. I don't need to tell you that your vision allows you to enjoy the shades of green grass as you watch your child play or the beaming smile on their face. But did you know that the visual system also works with those hidden senses so that your child can accomplish visual perceptual tasks such as completing puzzles or cutting a circle out of paper? The visual system plays a role in academic and coordination success. Vision goes beyond having 20/20 eyesight. In fact, a child can have perfect vision and still become dysregulated if there is too much visual input for them to process, interfering with sleep and their ability to pay attention.

When children struggle with visual input, it's a challenge for them and their parents. I want to tell you about a client, Alana, who even as a baby, would scream and shut her eyes whenever she was exposed to a lot of visual input—a busy environment, television, lots of movement. Her parents tried to calm her by getting close to her face or shaking rattles or toys in front of her, which only made it worse. Alana much preferred dark spaces with no visual input. She struggled with movement, too, and became carsick, so you can imagine how hard it was for her, living in LA, where little ones spend a lot of time sitting in their car seats. After a few months of intense sensory-integration work followed by weekly sessions, Alana is now thriving. Her case is an extreme one, but sometimes a fussy baby may have trouble processing sensory input, and you do not want to overload them by putting toys or yourself in their face. Children who are visually sensitive can even be overwhelmed by a colorful room.

Decorating with a riot of primary colors is common in nurseries, children's bedrooms, classrooms, and playrooms. As I've mentioned, I provide consultations to both schools and parents on how to organize a classroom and playroom; this is a big passion of mine, because it compromises our kids' ability to succeed when we overload their surroundings. So, before we jump any further into the visual system, I want to give you a few tips on minimizing visual input to keep your little one regulated and engaged.

At Play 2 Progress, we have nothing on the walls and decorate minimally. We don't use bright colors. We use muted hues as a foundation, with pops of bright colors for style. Our toy cabinets in the workrooms have doors on them so toys are concealed when they are not in action. In the gyms, every ball or game is put away in an opaque bin with a label. We also have fewer toys than you might think. We choose quality over quantity. Visual clutter can be distracting, and we want to avoid jumbled stacks of knickknacks, disorganized piles of papers, and scattered toys as much as possible.

CREATING A CALM SPACE

In order to create a space that is not overstimulating, here are some of the guidelines we follow at Play 2 Progress that you can adapt at home.

- **Place only a few things on the wall.**

    Posters, big neon paintings, mobiles, or knickknacks that crowd the walls, shelves, and floor contribute to visual clutter and distraction.

- **Use muted colors.**

    Keep the colors muted and calming; stay away from neon.

- **Set up the space so that all toys are hidden when put away.** Ideally, keep toys out of the bedroom altogether.

    If toys must be stored in the bedroom, keep them in an organized chest or storage box that can be closed. You might take a picture of the toys that will be stored together in a bin, and tape the picture on the top or side. Now your child can help with cleanup before they can read. IKEA makes an affordable, attractive toy storage unit.

- **Use warm, yellow-hued lighting.**

    Stay away from bright white fluorescent lights.

- **Embrace a minimalist style.**

    This is both my personal preference and far less stimulating for your little one.

CREATING A CALM CLASSROOM

- **Hang minimal posters and charts on the walls.**

    While the slogans on motivational posters may be inspirational, they tend to be overstimulating and add to dysregulation. Any extra charts (even the number line) on the walls also serve as visual clutter that should be minimized.

- **Don't use overstimulating signals.**

    A cowbell or flashing lights may be too overstimulating to signal a transition; instead try something soft like peace fingers or a gentle chime.

- **Keep bookshelves organized.**

  Keep book- and work shelves, as well as countertops and folder bins, organized and, if possible, out of sight from the kids' desks.

- **Use muted colors and stay within a color scheme.**

  The items that can be purchased at a school supply store are often bright and overstimulating; it is best to use muted colors and stay within a color scheme.

- **Build a calming corner.**

  Have a cozy area, possibly in a tent, where kids can go if they feel overstimulated to calm their body, read a book, and relax.

- **Have a work area with no stimulation.**

  Some kids, like adults, need an area to work without visual stimuli. Have a little cubicle where those who need a quieter space can go to do their work and focus.

From the minute most babies are born, they can see, but they can't yet distinguish all the details of vision that enhance our day-to-day lives. In the first three months of life, babies can see only high-contrast items like those in black and white, which is why there are so many black-and-white infant toys (and why we have a zebra in our set of Animagnets at Play 2 Progress). One behavior to look for in those first few months is if your baby is looking at and reacting to your face. When you gaze down and talk to your baby (who I'm sure is unbearably cute) and they smile back, that smile and coo are essential aspects of development. In our three-month-old Parent & Me classes, one of the first things we teach our parents is to get on their tummies so they can be face-to-face with their babies and then to slowly shift their bodies from side to side. If you do this at home, your babe should start to track you as you move. You can also see this reaction by slowly waving their beloved toy in front of them from one side to the other. They will track the toy with their eyes, which means that their eyes follow the object in a coordinated manner, rather than shaking their head from side to side. They will also develop their visual-processing skills as they play with a variety of toys and when they reach to grab for a toy hanging from their car seat or on their play mat. As they begin to crawl and become more active, they will really be able to explore their visual system and even more so as they start walking.

As occupational therapists, we look beyond 20/20—which is how most people think of the sense of vision—and consider other aspects of the system, including visual perception, oculomotor skills (tracking), visual motor integration skills, and hand-eye coordination.

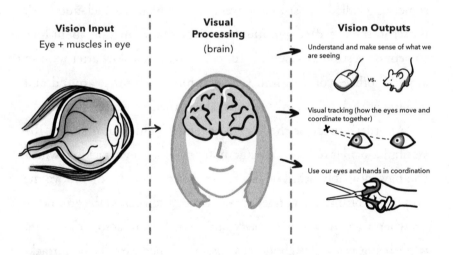

The Visual System

How the Visual System Works

I will leave the eye tests to the ophthalmologists and optometrists, and I won't bore you with the anatomy of the eye, as that is not my specialty. Instead, let's jump right into the information that you probably don't know about the visual system and how it impacts us all: how visual information is processed.

The vestibular sense works with the visual system to help a child do things like spin in dance class and read. Let's briefly review the vestibulo-ocular reflex, which links eyes to a moving body and allows us to steady our gaze when our head moves. It comes into play when a child looks between the board and the notes on their desk or spots their cheering parent in the crowd as they run the final yard in the cross-country race. If a child struggles with vestibulo-ocular reflex, even the small motions of their head while reading are challenging; you can imagine how this would impact them in school. We can test something called a post-rotary nystagmus, which is a back-and-forth flutter in the eye after spinning that gives us information about how someone's vestibular system is functioning. On a slow afternoon in any OT office, you can find OTs spinning each other around and looking at each other's eyes to learn about their vestibular systems.

Another aspect of the visual system is oculomotor skills. The vestibular-ocular reflex is an oculomotor skill, as is eye tracking, which you have probably heard of. There are six tiny muscles that move the eyes in a coordinated manner to watch a ball roll across the ground— or, when they grow older, check out a crush from across the room, while being as low-key about it as possible. When we talk about tracking skills, we are actually assessing how the eyes move and coordinate together. Think of what your child's face looks like when you are bringing a birthday cake to the table. They may be sitting in their chair, but their eyes are glued to that cake as it crosses their visual field; this is called a smooth pursuit. We also look at visual saccades, which are fast movements of the eyes that are like jumping, meaning the child isn't tracking or following one item, but instead quickly shifting their gaze around their environment. This type of sight is used when your child scans the playground to see where a friend has gone. Additional oculomotor skills are convergence, which permits the eyes to come together to view objects that are close to them, and divergence, which is when the eyes move slightly farther apart to take in objects that are in the distance.

It is also crucial for your child to better perceive and interact with their world in a number of ways. Let's start with visual attention. Visual attention has multiple components, including staying focused on what someone is doing. It allows children to concentrate on what they need to in any particular situation and to disregard the rest, like watching the teacher and ignoring what's outside the classroom window. It also enables them to divide their attention between two things, like kicking a soccer ball while keeping an eye on the goal.

Visual perception is our ability to understand and make sense of what we are seeing. A child can have perfect vision and still struggle with visual perception, which can have a detrimental impact on academics and sports. Here are the key components of visual perception:

1. Figure ground—the ability to spot a figure among its background (like finding Waldo).
2. Visual memory—this is exactly what it sounds like: the ability to remember what they have seen. This is when a child remembers what a shape looks like in order to draw it.
3. Visual closure—being able to perceive a whole without seeing the entire image. So, if a corner of that triangle puzzle piece is hiding under the couch, they can see part of it and know it is the piece they need.

4. Form constancy—this is the skill to recognize an item even if it is in a different form (e.g., upside down or at an angle). That same puzzle piece can now be flipped and your little one should still recognize it is a triangle.

5. Visual sequential memory—when they can remember visual items in the correct order. This is important for when a child needs to write their phone number or do math.

6. Visual spatial relationships—this is the capacity to understand where objects are in space. This includes understanding directions like "in front" or "on top," and impacts depth perception. It also contributes to a sense of direction and allows children to write with proper spacing.

7. Visual discrimination—this is the ability to tell the difference between objects, particularly those with subtle differences, like "p" versus "q" or "b" versus "d."

• • •

When your kid is copying a triangle or their name, they first have to use visual perception to perceive the triangle and letters and then use that information in tandem with their fine motor skills to write. Copying from the board is a visual motor skill and you can imagine what a critical role these skills play in day-to-day life and academic success.

I also hear a lot of parents talk about hand-eye coordination, but for some reason, they don't associate it with our visual sense; it is seen as more rooted in physicality. But hand-eye coordination has everything to do with how the eyes guide a child to do everything from grasping a rattle to hitting a tennis ball with a racquet. The goal is for the eyes and hands to coordinate smoothly and fluidly to catch and throw that Frisbee in the backyard or bead a necklace for mom.

I can't say it enough: a child can have perfect vision and still have a visual-processing disorder. That means that they have trouble with how their brain processes the information they see using the skills that I've just described. You may notice your little one flips their letters, has trouble copying shapes, or their letter spacing is too close, too far, too small, or too big. Remember that when children are first learning to write, it is common for them to flip a few of those letters and write far too big, too small, or unevenly. We want to see those inconsistencies start to fade at about seven years old.

Key Aspects of Visual Sense

Visual discrimination: This is your child's ability to distinguish small differences between objects, such as an "m" and an "n" or a "b" or a "d." Also, it supports their understanding of where objects are in relation to one another, paying attention to what is important on the page, distinguishing background from foreground, remembering what they saw and the order it was in (think of the game Memory), and figuring out what they are looking at even if they see only a part of the item. If a child has trouble discriminating visually, school will be a challenge every day.

I also want to mention it is important that your child experience the world by physically doing things that develop visual discrimination. This is how they learn about the qualities of what they are interacting with. For example, a child needs to experience playing with a ball to fully appreciate that it is three-dimensional, has weight, a shape, and so on; playing with a ball on a screen doesn't allow them to recognize all the properties of a ball. If they have an opportunity to play with a ball, when they see a picture of it later, they will understand that it is a three-dimensional object.

Visual modulation: Some kids are over-responsive to visual stimuli, which means they might have trouble in bright lights and squint. They may become distracted by their classmates moving around, multiple colorful posters, and visual clutter. They can also be under-responsive to visual stimuli and seek input, including wanting to look at bright lights or spinning objects.

Visual Activities

Matching Monarch

Description: This craft will leave you with a beautiful butterfly ready to take off.

Materials:
- Paper
- Markers or colored pencils

Space: Small

Time: 10–15 minutes

Setup: See the illustration for a butterfly that you can copy, or make your own. Be as creative as you want. Fold a piece of paper in half, and draw a butterfly wing on one side of the paper. Your child will duplicate what you have drawn on the other side, so keep it simple. You don't have to make it look like a "real" butterfly—just be sure to use a number of shapes that your child can draw and color in on their half of the butterfly.

Directions

Step 1: Make sure your little one is seated at the table with their feet on the ground. An empty table is always better to minimize visual distraction.

Step 2: Explain that butterflies are symmetrical—that one side will match the other—and that you have drawn and colored one wing, but it is their job to draw and color the other.

Step 3: Ask your child to complete the butterfly, making sure it matches the side of the butterfly that you drew.

Step 4: They color the butterfly so both sides match.

Make it a little easier: Instead of asking your little one to draw and color the butterfly wing, draw the entire butterfly and have them match the colors from one wing to the other.

Make it a little harder: Add multiple patterns and additional shapes that your little one will need to match.

Additional Skills: Fine Motor

Dizzy Animals

1+2   3+4   5   6+7

Description: This is a big challenge, but it is also really fun, so kids don't even realize how hard they are working.

Materials:
- Animal drawings: Use large images that you print out from the web or use photos cut from magazines.

Space: Large

Time: 10–15 minutes

Setup: Make sure you have a big open space, and stack the animal drawings into a pile.

Directions

Step 1: Stand on the opposite side of the space from your little one.
Step 2: Have them get down on the ground into a log roll position.
Step 3: Hold up the animal pictures one at a time.
Step 4: They start rolling toward you.
Step 5: As they roll, have them tell you what animal you are holding up without stopping.
Step 6: Continuously change from one animal to the next in the stack so they have to focus on you and identify the animal, all while rolling.
Step 7: Repeat the same task as they roll away from you.

Make it a little easier: Change the animal slowly. Give them a few rolls before switching to the next one.

Make it a little harder: Use letters instead of animals. Hold up a sequence of letters and have them read them out loud.

Additional Skills: Vestibular

Junk Drawer Jewels

Description: This easy exercise requires only a little space and whatever you can find in your desk drawer.

Materials:
- A bin filled with a few very small random items (paper clips, erasers, pencils)
- Large beads
- String or pipe cleaners

Space: Small

Time: 10–15 minutes

Setup: Dump the beads into the bin and put the string or pipe cleaners on the side.

Directions

Step 1: Ask your little one to make you (or themselves) a necklace.
Step 2: They reach into the bin (looking into it) and pick out the beads from among the other items.
Step 3: They slip the beads onto the string.
Step 4: Tie the necklace and put it on.

Make it a little easier: Add only a few small items in the bin with all the beads.

Make it a little harder: Add a timer. How quickly can your child find the beads?

Baby Bonus Activity: Hide their favorite toys to find in a bin of other items.

Additional Skills: Fine Motor

Shape Shuffle

Description: This is a variation on the game Memory with an added challenge. You can play it with tangrams or any toys you have around the house.

Materials:
- Ten shapes in a variety of colors or ten small toys

Space: Small

Time: 15–20 minutes

Setup: Mix up the shapes and choose five.

Directions

Step 1: Put the five shapes in a row to create a sequence.

Step 2: Let your child have thirty seconds to look at the sequence.

Step 3: Let your child shuffle the shapes.

Step 4: Ask your child to put them back in order.

Step 5: Mix up a different group of shapes and repeat.

Make it a little easier: Start with three shapes instead of five.

Make it a little harder: When you mix up the shapes after your child has had a chance to examine the sequence, toss in some extra shapes so they need to pick from more than five. You can also add some that are the same shape but are a different color.

Additional Skills: Praxis

Zoo Escape

Description: The animals have escaped, and only your child can find them!

Materials:
- Small toy animals or stuffed animals

Space: Medium

Time: 10–15 minutes

Setup: Hide the animals throughout the room so only parts of them are visible. Try under the bed, in a half-opened drawer with a head peeking out, and so on.

Directions

Step 1: Tell your child that the animals are hiding from all the zookeepers, and they need to find them.

Step 2: Give them a mission—for example, "Find the zebra first!"

Step 3: Continue until all the animals are found.

Step 4: Return the animals to the zoo (a box or container).

Make it a little easier: Have a little more of each animal showing in their hiding places.

Make it a little harder: Choose animals that are the same color and have similar appearance.

Baby Bonus Activity: Hide their favorite toys under a blanket with a bit poking out and have them find them.

Additional Skills: Proprioception

LEGO Sort

1   2   3

Description: Turn cleanup into a game. Nothing makes me happier than an organized LEGO bin.

Materials:
- LEGO pieces
- Three bins
- Timer

Space: Medium

Time: 10–15 minutes

Setup: Put the LEGO pieces in a pile with the three bins on the floor.

Directions

Step 1: Tell your little one that you are going to play a game and see how fast they can sort their LEGO pieces. Explain that they need to separate them by size so the small LEGO pieces will go in one bin, the medium in another, and the large ones in the last.

Step 2: Start the timer for five minutes and say "GO!"

Step 3: After the five minutes are up, check to see that the LEGO pieces were put in the correct bin.

Make it a little easier: Forget the timer. Let them sort at their own pace.

Make it a little harder: Can they choose LEGO pieces that are only slightly different in shape (e.g., two, three, and four rows of pegs, all the same color)?

Baby Bonus Activity: Container play is the best. Can they help you put Cheerios in one bowl and fruit in the other?

Additional Skills: Fine Motor

Loopy Letters

1   2   3

Description: This one is for any child struggling with letters and writing their name. They often enjoy spelling their parents' and siblings' names as well.

Materials:
- Pipe cleaners or Wikki Stix

Space: Small

Time: 15–20 minutes

Setup: Bend the pipe cleaners or Wikki Stix into the letters of your child's name.

Directions

Step 1: Mix up the letters on the table, with some upside down and reversed.

Step 2: Ask your little one to rearrange the pipe cleaners to spell out their name.

Step 3: Repeat with additional letters and names.

Make it a little easier: Make sure all letters are right side up and in the correct orientation, just not in order.

Make it a little harder: Mix in letters that don't appear in their name.

Additional Skills: Tactile

Silly Spiders

1   2   3

Description: This activity works well outside, or with paper and markers if you are stuck inside on a rainy day.

Materials:
- Chalk
- Markers
- Paper

Space: Large

Time: 10–15 minutes

Setup: Draw a few spiders on one side of the driveway and a few webs on the other side. Then draw loopy pathways that go from each spider to a web. **Rainy-Day Version:** Use markers on paper to make the spiders, their webs, and their paths.

Directions

Step 1: Explain to your little one that the spiders can't find their way back to their web.

Step 2: Have them choose a spider to lead to their web. With their chalk (or marker), they draw a line from spider to web along the path you created.

Step 3: Repeat for all the spiders.

Make it a little easier: Make the paths straight instead of looped or diagonal.

Make it a little harder: Don't make the paths direct. Maybe the top spider loops its way to the bottom web rather than the first spider going to the first web and so on.

Additional Skills: Fine Motor

Builder and Architect

Description: I came up with this game in my first year as an occupational therapist and have been playing it with my kiddos ever since.

Materials:
- Magna-Tiles or any building blocks

Space: Medium

Time: 20–30 minutes

Setup: Build a structure out of Magna-Tiles.

Directions

Step 1: Tell your little one that they are the architect and need to re-create the structure you built and that they will need to tell you or another child how to build it.

Important rule: The architect cannot touch the building materials and the builder has to follow all of the architect's directions.

Step 2: Have the architect start explaining how to build the building (e.g., "Put the red Magna-Tile on the blue one and then put the yellow next to the red.").

Step 3: Continue until your at-home Taj Mahal has been built.

Step 4: Switch places so each person gets a chance to be builder and architect.

Make it a little easier: Build a simple tower so that the instructions are easier to give. For example, say, "Stack the blue Magna-Tile on top of the pink one."

Make it a little harder: Build a complex structure.

Baby Bonus Activity: Show your little one how to stack blocks or place them in a bucket.

Additional Skills: Praxis

Tower Tumble

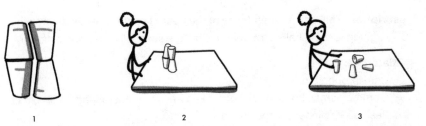

Description: Break this out at a picnic or any time you need to shake things up a little. It is actually quite difficult, but the challenge is hidden in the fun.

Materials:
- Six to eight plastic cups, any size

Space: Small

Time: 10–15 minutes

Setup: No setup necessary

Directions

Step 1: Build a tower using the cups. Get creative—make a pyramid, stack the cups so they are resting opening to opening, or design a cup house.

Step 2: Let your little one have one minute to look at what you built and remember how to build it.

Step 3: Knock over the tower and have them rebuild it.

Make it a little easier: Make a tower using only three or four cups.

Make it a little harder: Add a time limit. Can they rebuild the structure in thirty seconds?

Baby Bonus Activity: Stack items like blocks and have your baby imitate you. You can also do this with a ring stacker.

Additional Skills: Proprioception

Shake 'n' Seek

Description: This game reminds me of the hours I spent when I was growing up searching for seashells on a beach. Now the seashell hunt comes indoors.

Materials:
- See-through bin
- Common small household items, like pencils, markers, paper clips, hair ties, LEGO pieces, or toy animals
- Sand (or rice)

Space: Small

Time: 10–15 minutes

Setup: Pour the sand into the bin and hide the items. It should be deep enough to mostly cover them.

Directions

Step 1: Hand the bin to your child.
Step 2: Have them gently shake it from side to side.
Step 3: As they shake and the items poke out from the sand, ask them if they can name what they see.
Step 4: Have them continue shaking the bin until they name everything inside.

Make it a little easier: Hide bigger items.

Make it a little harder: Add a time limit and do not let them stop shaking. No stopping to take a closer look!

Additional Skills: Proprioceptive

Popsicle-Stick Spelling

Description: Every child learns differently, and some struggle to master their letters if they solely copy them down. They can benefit from using manipulatives to create their letters before putting pencil to paper.

Materials:
- Popsicle sticks
- Glue
- Paper
- Finger paint

Space: Small

Time: 20–25 minutes

Setup: Set everything out on the table. Write your little one's name or a shape on the paper. Make the lines large enough to act as a guide for where they will put the Popsicle sticks.

Directions

Step 1: Tell them to put glue along the lines of their name or shape on the paper: "Trace the letters or shape in glue!" I suggest letting them dip their finger directly in the glue.

Step 2: Have your child place the Popsicle sticks along the lines to make the letters.

Step 3: They can then dip their fingers in paint and color the Popsicle sticks.

Make it a little easier: Glue on the Popsicle sticks for them and then ask them to finger-paint the Popsicle sticks. They will still be tracing the letters as they do it.

Make it a little harder: Don't prewrite their name; have them do that from the start.

Additional Skills: Tactile, Fine Motor

Figure 8 Track

1   2   3

Description: As you may have gathered by now, OTs love using the figure 8 in a variety of ways. Writing the infinity symbol can be tricky, so rather than having kids trace "∞," it's time to get inventive.

Materials:
- Paint—chalk paint if outside, and nontoxic water-based paint if inside
- Plates (one for each color of paint)
- Paper
- Toy car

Space: Medium

Time: 10–15 minutes

Setup: Draw a double-sided figure 8 (see illustration). Pour paint onto a plate, one plate for each color.

Directions

Step 1: Have your child roll the car through the paint until the wheels are covered.

Step 2: They roll the car over the figure 8 or infinity symbol two or three times, until it has been fully painted.

Step 3: Repeat with more colors.

Make it a little easier: Draw arrows that your child can follow while rolling over the symbol.

Make it a little harder: Have your little one draw the initial figure 8.

Baby Bonus Activity: Draw a straight path and let your kiddo roll the car on the path with the paint.

Additional Skills: Tactile

Monster Mash

1   2   3

Description: Break this one out in airports, during car rides, and in restaurants—anywhere a kid is likely to get bored while waiting around. All you need is paper and a pen or marker, and you can play as many times as you want to pass the time.

Materials:
- Pens or markers
- Paper

Space: Small

Time: 20–25 minutes

Setup: Draw two identical monster heads, including details like hair, nose, mouth, cheeks, and freckles. Draw a third monster that looks almost the same as the other two, but with one to three small differences.

Directions

Step 1: Give your little one the paper and pen/marker and allow them to look at the monsters.

Step 2: Ask them to spot all the differences and mark them when they find them.

Step 3: Repeat with more monsters.

Make it a little easier: Make the differences more obvious, like curly versus straight hair, button nose versus line nose, or sad versus smiling mouth.

Make it a little harder: Hide those differences. Try four freckles instead of five, oval eyes versus circle eyes, and so on.

Additional Skills: Fine Motor

Additional Visual Activities

You probably play some of these already but may not have known they were tools for developing the visual system.

Backyard/outdoor games
- Drawing with chalk
- Hanging a ball on a string from a tree and hitting it
- Hopscotch
- I Spy
- Keeping a non-helium balloon up

Board and other games
- Spot It!
- Guess Who?
- Where's Waldo?
- Mental Blox
- Tricky Hands
- Tangrams
- Rush Hour
- Connect Four
- Puzzles
- Coloring books
- Arts and crafts

6

A LITTLE TASTE

Waking Up the Gustatory System

. . . .

The gustatory sense, otherwise known as taste, was another challenge while I was growing up (are you beginning to sense a theme when it comes to my sensory system?). For a long time—well, through early adulthood—I stuck to a diet of buttered noodles and mac 'n' cheese. It wasn't until I was in the middle of OT school that I truly understood how amazing this sense was and that it was time to diversify my plate. I forced myself to try new foods, one bite at a time. Now, I'm proud to say that I am a total foodie.

When you think of your childhood, your culture, your vacations, and your daily plans, food often plays a leading role. Eating helps us bond, reminds us of family, and provides comfort and a reason to gather together. I don't need to tell you just how essential the sense of taste is to everyday life. It creates community and conversation and is a reason to travel across town and around the world. For your child, it's an opportunity to go to the park with their best buddies to chow down on pizza or a sweet treat, eat at a friend's house, enjoy dinner out with family, and share snack time with classmates.

Our ability to appreciate food and flavors actually comes from the senses of smell and taste working together. Another key point is that taste is different from flavor. For the sake of simplicity, we are going to jump in to talking about food, but keep in mind that flavor is influenced by taste, texture, temperature, and smell, and we will get into those nuances later in the chapter and in the olfactory chapter.

When the phone rings in our office, it's not uncommon for it to be a panicked parent whose little one will not eat a variety of foods. This usually goes beyond preferring bland foods, keeping foods separate on their plate, or refusing to eat anything with pepper—those aversions are common. But picky eating is a problem when a child will eat only one food, like chicken nuggets, at the expense of everything else. The limits of what they are willing to put in their mouth makes it impossible to eat outside their home, at a friend's, or at school. As someone who did not learn the joys of food until I was an adult, I am passionate about helping children diversify their palates from the get-go—while keeping realistic expectations. Yes, some kids will happily down sushi and spicy curries, especially if they grow up in households in which a range of cuisines are offered. But many—especially those who are used to a relatively bland Standard American Diet— stick to turkey sandwiches, pasta, rice, and chicken. It's OK for your child to have preferences, as we all do—but when what they eat (or won't eat) gets in the way of mealtime, family time, or time with friends, it may be the right moment to make some changes.

Over the years, many children have come to Play 2 Progress to deal with picky eating, but I always think of one little boy, Rocco.

Rocco attended our summer camp and at snack time wanted his plate filled with the same food as his friends, but he would never even take a bite. His extreme sensitivity went beyond taste to involve smell and texture—a prime example of how the senses work together to impact food preferences. He could taste the difference between his mom's homemade tomato sauce and store-bought and could not tolerate anything but Mom's. Otherwise, Rocco was exclusively willing to eat dino nuggets, Tostitos tortilla chips, American cheese slices, and Jif crunchy peanut butter. This presented a big issue at birthday parties, both at his own and especially at other kids', because he wouldn't eat anything except these specific *brands*. He was embarrassed to bring his own food, but he would also refuse the food at a friend's house. The only option was to keep the playdates short to avoid a meal and make sure that the host parents knew about his preferences and didn't try to give Rocco a snack. We slowly expanded his diet by building off his preferred foods to try something similar. Although at six he is still not an adventurous eater, he can now eat meals like spaghetti that are not prepared at home and has even recently started eating pizza—a huge step in being comfortable at birthday parties and on playdates.

Taste is fascinating, including in how it develops. Starting in utero, the flavors the birth mother eats make it through the amniotic fluid, so the fetus is exposed to those tastes. Once a baby is born, if they are breastfed, the flavors in the breast milk are likewise shared, helping them develop a preference for particular foods. This is one of the reasons why it is critical for a mom to eat a well-balanced diet during pregnancy and while nursing. Babies have a preference for sweet foods that mimic the high sugar content of breast milk, which explains why they may gravitate to foods that are not necessarily nutritious, but with exposure to healthy foods starting in pregnancy, they can maintain an inclination toward a diet that is less likely to lead to obesity, diabetes, and many other issues. That's why when a baby begins on solids, it is important to introduce them to as many foods as possible so that they'll be more likely to stick with a healthy diet. Kids may resist trying something unfamiliar, but that doesn't necessarily mean they are picky eaters, just that their taste buds are developing. Don't give up. It can take many times before they will consistently eat, accept, and like a new food. Again, we're talking about taste in terms of the gustatory system, but remember that texture and especially smell are also closely involved in food preferences.

Because what kids like to eat is based on early exposure to those foods, you can see how culture and what your family eats has an impact on them as an adult. My personal experience is once again a prime example. My mom is extremely picky and does not eat any food that is mushy or soft—ever. This includes mashed potatoes, dressing on salad, or food with any sauce. She tends to stick to bland foods but also has a sweet tooth. My dad could not imagine a meal that didn't include a big slab of meat. All in all, we ate a typical American diet (also known as the Standard American Diet, or SAD) that was actually pretty unhealthy. If you saw what my parents ate at an average dinner—large portions of meat and potatoes, bread, and dessert— you would think they didn't care about their health, but they worked out all the time. In fact, my mom owned a fitness company and my dad was an avid athlete. So, while I grew up around people who exercised, mealtimes were another story. I was offered very few foods with strong flavors and rarely ate anything with a soft texture, with the exception of pasta or a baked potato. I don't think I ate a salad until grad school. It wasn't until I studied sensory processing that I truly began to understand my food preferences. I also realized I could change them. With that said, when I am having a hard day, nothing comforts me more than mac 'n' cheese (although these days I go for a vegan version).

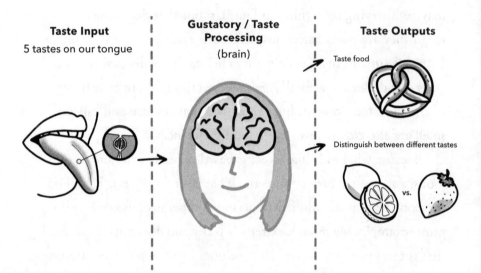

Taste Input
5 tastes on our tongue

Gustatory / Taste Processing
(brain)

Taste Outputs
Taste food

Distinguish between different tastes

vs.

The Gustatory System

How the Gustatory System Works

We have the ability to identify five basic tastes on our tongue: sweet, sour, bitter, salty, and umami (savory). The taste goes from the food to the taste buds, which are each sensitive to one of those tastes, and from the taste buds to the brain, where the signals combine with other sensory information, including smell, which has a major impact on food preferences (which we'll discuss in the next chapter). As I know both from personal experience and from working with kids like Rocco, it is possible, through consistent exposure to new foods, to expand a child's preferences.

INTRODUCING NEW FOODS

Because picky eating is such a common concern for parents, here are a few strategies for broadening your child's diet.

- **Offer the food without an expectation that they will eat it.**

  It can take many introductions of a food before a little one will show interest. Forcing them can backfire in a big way.

- **Allow them to get silly and let them play with the food before eating it.**

  Use broccoli as a paintbrush and make veggie paint (see page 93).

  Build houses with celery (see page 95).

- **Take the pressure off.**

  Don't use bribes of dessert or a preferred activity if only they eat the food.

  To decrease their concern over eating a food and to reduce any pressure, let them know that if they give it a try, they can always spit it out if they want to.

- **Before asking them to try it, set an example and eat it yourself.** Talk about how delicious it is.

  Compare it to foods they like: "Wow, this carrot is the same color as mac 'n' cheese and it is crunchy like Cheddar Bunnies."

- **Eat family style.**

  Technology-free, family-style dinners are a way to present new foods.

- **Get creative.**

  A change in environment, like a backyard picnic, makes eating more fun and can increase their willingness to be adventurous. Or set up a picnic blanket in the living room.

Because taste preferences start even before birth, I am passionate about advising parents to watch out for added sugars in formula. Infants are impacted by what they are exposed to during those first months of life. Through breast milk, they experience the flavors that their mother has eaten and will likely feed the child once they wean, and whether you're breastfeeding or formula feeding, it's better if babies are not overexposed to sugar, which is already their natural preference. All humans have an instinct to be wary of bitter foods, likely because most poisonous foods are also bitter; it's an inherited trait to protect us. However, most veggies contain at least a hint of bitterness, so it's helpful to work on overcoming this natural tendency. Foods that your kid dislikes at first can turn into favorites. Again: children should be exposed to vegetables early and often so they learn to accept and like them and build the foundations for a healthy diet.

A child needs to be able to discriminate between tastes and to modulate. This means not gagging on foods and not seeking out super spicy tastes, either. Much of being over-responsive, under-responsive, or having trouble discriminating taste involves other sensory systems, too. In case I haven't said it enough, picky eating is driven by smell, taste, temperature, and texture, not an isolated sense of taste.

Key Aspects of Gustatory Sense

Gustatory discrimination: This is the ability to distinguish among the tastes. In order for your child to enjoy their food, they need to be able to tell if a food is sweet, sour, bitter, salty, or umami, and that is where discrimination comes into play. Speaking of play, the activities in this chapter encourage your child to have fun with their food—bending the rules a little to avoid picky eating.

Gustatory modulation: This is the ability to have the just-right reaction to taste. Remember, having an appropriate response to foods involves both our sense of smell and our sense of taste. Children who struggle with this may crave intense flavors and dislike bland food. Or they may be picky eaters who avoid strong flavors and reject foods to the point that doing so interferes with their daily life.

Gustatory Activities

A Feast of Color

1   2   3

Description: Getting your little one to try new foods can be challenging. A great way to experiment with new tastes is to encourage them to play with their food. Remember, never force your child to try anything. Show them that you are having fun trying the flavors and they can copy what you do if they would like to. (For more painting with food, see Veggie Finger Paint on page 93.)

Materials:
- A variety of colored foods (berries work well, as do condiments and spices such as cinnamon)
- Small bowls
- Water
- A spoon for mixing your "paints"
- Clean and sanitary paintbrush (your child must be able to eat off it, so I suggest using a new one)
- Paper or a paper plate

Space: Small

Time: 15–20 minutes

Setup: Place small amounts of each food in the bowls.

Directions

Step 1: To make the paint, crush your berries or spices, add a little water, and stir. The consistency won't be an ideal "paint" texture, and it's OK even if it is chunky. If you prefer, you can put the "veggie paint" in the blender to make it smoother.

Step 2: Give your child the paintbrush and let them start painting.

Step 3: Allow them to play while painting and taste some of the paint. If you paint on a plate, your child can lick it off. You can also encourage your little one to paint with their fingers and hands.

Make it a little easier: Make the paints for your little one and let them paint.

Make it a little harder: Forget the paintbrush and have them paint with their hands.

Additional Skills: Fine Motor, Tactile

Blind Taste Test

Description: Explore the five tastes—sweet, sour, salty, bitter, and umami—while also introducing some tastes that your child may normally avoid. Keeping it light and easy is key.

Materials:
- One sour, sweet, salty, bitter, and umami food. I like using lemon slices, sugar cubes, Himalayan salt, unsweetened cacao nibs, and seaweed or salmon jerky (any jerky will do).
- Cupcake tin
- Blindfold

Space: Small

Time: 5–10 minutes

Setup: Place a little of each food in the cupcake tin (one item per cupcake holder).

Directions

Step 1: Teach your little one about the five tastes. You could say, "We have five different tastes that we can taste. They are sour like lemon, bitter like lettuce, umami like soy sauce, sweet like candy, and salty like pretzels." You can also name the foods and point to where they are in the cupcake tin as you explain.

Step 2: Put the blindfold on your child.

Step 3: Give them the first spoon, and ask them to taste the food.

Step 4: After they have tasted, remove the blindfold.

Step 5: Ask them to guess what food they tried and which of the five tastes it is. They can point to the correct space in the cupcake tin.

Make it a little easier: Forget the blindfold.

Make it a little harder: Keep the blindfold on and have them guess without looking at the foods in front of them.

Baby Bonus Activity: Put a tiny bit of the five different tastes on their tongue to let them see how they react to the taste.

Additional Skills: Proprioception

Chocolate Challenge

Description: When I started to enjoy cooking and moved to more of a plant-based diet, I found it fascinating that cocoa in its natural form is quite bitter. In this activity, your little ones will explore the ways that cocoa can be made to taste. It is also a terrific way to start teaching about added sugar and nutrition.

Materials:
- ½ cup unsweetened chocolate chips
- ½ cup agave or maple syrup
- About ½ tablespoon salt
- Bowls
- Microwave
- Spoons for tasting

Space: Small

Time: 15–20 minutes

Setup: Place the unsweetened chocolate chips in a microwavable bowl. Place a small bowl of agave or maple syrup and a small bowl of salt on the table. You aren't about to make dessert (although if you want to do that after, go for it), so no need for perfection. The purpose here is to give your little one the opportunity to explore their taste buds.

Directions

Step 1: Both you and your child taste the unsweetened chocolate chips and talk about their bitter taste. This is not the yummy chocolate we are used to. Explain that the familiar chocolate taste comes from adding sugar.

Step 2: Melt the unsweetened chocolate in the bowl with the agave or maple syrup in the microwave, stirring at fifteen-to-twenty-second intervals until it is melted and smooth. Once it has cooled, taste the chocolate and talk about how adding the sugar made it sweet.

Step 3: Take the melted chocolate you just made and add the salt. If it has hardened, microwave to melt it again, stir to combine, and discuss how the salt changed the taste.

Make it a little easier: Pre-make all three versions of chocolate (unsweetened, sweet, and salted) and have them taste the difference.

Make it a little harder: Pre-make the chocolates and have them guess which is which.

Additional Skills: Olfactory

Smooth Tasting

Description: Kids enjoy being involved in the process of preparing their own food, and making a smoothie is an easy way to get them involved while creating a nutritious treat.

Materials:
- 1½ cups fruit of your choice. I suggest letting your little one pick which ones, and I always toss in a banana for extra sweetness (if you use a frozen banana, omit the ice).
- 1 cup cow's milk or nut milk of your choice, more if needed once blended
- ½ cup ice
- Blender
- Drinking cups
- 1 cup vegetable of their choice (I use spinach) (optional)

Space: Small

Time: 10–15 minutes

Setup: Place all the ingredients on a kid-size table or an area where your little one is able to reach.

Directions

Step 1: Tell your child that they get to make their own smoothie.

Step 2: Let them choose their amounts and combinations. It may be hard not to comment, but let them choose what goes into the blender, even if it seems unappetizing to you.

Step 3: Add milk and ice, and let your little one push the button to blend.

Step 4: Pour into cups and enjoy your smoothie.

Make it a little easier: Pre-measure all the ingredients.

Make it a little harder: Ask them to add at least one veggie to their smoothie (I suggest spinach, which doesn't add a super strong taste).

Additional Skills: Auditory

Straight-Faced Lemon

Description: Do you remember taking the Warhead challenge as a child? You had to eat the sour candy while keeping a straight face. Play it with a lemon instead of candy and get ready to laugh.

Materials:
- Lemon
- Bowl or plate
- Sugar

Space: Small

Time: 5 minutes

Setup: Peel a lemon, remove the seeds, and cut it into tiny pieces. Place the pieces in a bowl or on a plate.

Directions

Step 1: Challenge your little one to eat a piece of the lemon without making a face.
Step 2: Let them take a piece of the lemon and try it.
Step 3: Try it yourself.
Step 4: Who can keep a straight face?!

Make it a little easier: Add something sweet to the lemon, like some sugar on top.

Make it a little harder: Take a bigger piece of lemon.

Baby Bonus Activity: Let your toddler lick a lemon. Be sure to record them for their reaction!

Additional Skills: Olfactory

Additional Gustatory Activities

Food should be fun, not stressful. Every mealtime is an opportunity to teach your child about new flavors and foods.

- Expose, expose, expose. Remember that it takes many, many exposures for your little one to accept a new food. Start young and introduce tons of unfamiliar foods.
- Let your child in the kitchen to cook with you. Let them taste the ingredients. Give them a before-and-after taste test. Have them try a carrot or broccoli before it is cooked and then after.
- Go to a restaurant or a market that features foods from other cultures.

SCENT-SATIONAL

Getting the Olfactory System Engaged

. . . .

The olfactory sense, otherwise known as smell, can take us back in time, get our stomachs rumbling, comfort us, and have us running from the room sending accusing looks at whoever dealt it. It can alert us to an emergency, like when a candle tips over and starts a fire. It can also protect us from eating something that doesn't smell right, like milk that has gone bad. The amount of insight we gain from our sense of smell is often overlooked. Many people don't realize how it is able to elicit a memory, enhance the flavor of what we are eating, and soothe us when we are troubled. When a child is transitioning to sleeping in their own bed and is struggling with falling asleep without their parents, I advise the parents to give them a pillow from their bed or one of the parents' old T-shirts to snuggle with. The scent that lingers on the pillow or clothes can help a child feel comforted as they learn to sleep on their own. I also suggest that when you drop off your little one at preschool for the first time or at their first sleepover, give them something that carries your comforting scent. A shirt or pillow for naptime or even a scrunchie of yours that they wear on their wrist can do the trick.

Among the first scents we encounter are those of our moms. An infant can recognize the smell of their birth mother's milk, and it can even soothe them and ease their pain after a heel prick at their first doctor's visit. Only mom's milk has that ability.

Exposing a child to lots of smells from the time they are born will expand their diet and will also make them familiar with a wider range of scents, so they do not react negatively to them in a classroom or at a friend's house. Each new environment will have unfamiliar smells, some enjoyable, others less so. Liking one fragrance over another is often a matter of preference, but if a child hasn't been exposed to a range of smells, many scents they encounter will be off-putting or overwhelming. Just by engaging in the environment, most kids are exposed to a variety. Start young by adding cooked veggies into a secured mesh pouch and let your baby smell and explore.

Our sense of smell is the one most closely related to memory, because the olfactory system has a straight pathway to the areas of our brain that handle emotion. A smell will elicit different emotions in different people. As I'm sure you know, the scents of your childhood will quickly bring back memories, good and bad. Five or six years ago, I was browsing a store for a new body wash, smelling each to decide if it was the winner. I picked up one, opened it, and brought it to my nose. Suddenly, my heart cracked open and all of these old memories came flooding in. For the first time in years, in the scent of that body wash, I smelled my dad. That unexpected smell forced me to face pieces of the grief that I had buried since he had passed years earlier, and the rush of memories was both overwhelming and comforting.

Much like taste, every culture and family unit have their own unique smells, which become part of our identities and provide us with comfort in our most vulnerable times. When I was a child, my mom had an affinity for air freshener plug-ins, specifically the apple-cinnamon kind. Recently I found myself putting one in my shopping cart, despite how much I loathe those toxic things, because I was feeling nervous and needed a reminder of my Midwestern childhood, when life was just a little slower. That shot of apple-cinnamon gave me the comfort I needed. At Play 2 Progress, we make essential oil sprays with kids and pair them with a soothing memory to help them get through a hard time. We have also made monster repellent, calming sprays, and alerting sprays for those hard-to-wake-up mornings (see page 157).

You're not going to find a lot of Pinterest boards talking about smell and sensory play. Luckily, we have an activity that gets those ever-popular rice bins smelling great, for a double sensory boost—see page 158.

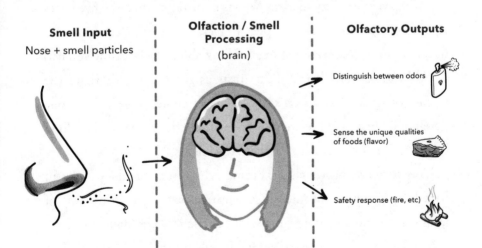

The Olfactory System

How the Olfactory System Works

When you put your nose up to a freshly bloomed flower on a crisp spring day and inhale, tiny molecules carrying the odor go through your nose and onto the olfactory bulb via a nerve signal. From there, the signal is passed to different areas of the brain, including the limbic system, which is the emotional control center. This is why memories and emotions emerge when the smell of hot chocolate brings you back to holidays at Grandma's house, and it's what led me to tears in the body wash aisle. It's also why your little one gets so excited the minute they smell their favorite cookies.

When an infant is born, they can already discriminate between smells. They have an affinity for their own mother's breast while nursing and can differentiate between their mother's scent and another woman's. Likewise, your baby's smell elicits your own hormones, particularly oxytocin.

We have the ability to identify tons more odors than the five tastes that were noted in the last chapter. In fact, food gets its dimension in flavor because of our sense of smell. Think about the last time you had a bad head cold; food just didn't taste as good as usual. That's the impact of sense of smell on taste. When it comes to your little one developing their own preferences, giving them the time to smell a food before eating it can encourage them to explore.

We currently have a client, Emma, who is social and a wonderful friend, but her sense of smell is so sensitive that it gets in the way of family time and spending time with her friends. Her dad can't cook vegetables or even eat cooked vegetables when Emma is in the kitchen or at the dinner table. At school, Emma cannot eat inside in the lunchroom because the smells of the other kids' lunches are distressing, and instead she has to eat outside at the picnic tables or in another room. Because she can't tolerate the smells of the lunchroom, Emma is also missing out on the socialization that happens there. We have slowly helped Emma get used to a variety of odors by playing with a number of scents. Now she can handle having foods in the same room with her, and we are working on getting her to sit at the table.

Key Aspects of Olfactory Sense

Olfactory discrimination: This is our ability to distinguish among the smells that we encounter every day—those we like and those we don't. What's more, the power of this sense is evident in infancy—a breast-feeding baby will be able to tell the difference between their mom and another woman. The nose knows!

Olfactory modulation: Just as it is with our other senses, olfactory modulation is the ability to have the just-right reaction to smell. Some children, like Emma, have a hard time tolerating certain smells, which can have a negative impact on their social lives, because restaurants, cafeterias, and classrooms are filled with a host of aromas. A little one who is over-responsive to a smell may gag or their eyes may water when they're hit with a certain smell. On the flip side, an under-responsive child may not smell subtle odors and be attracted to strong smells, including ones that their peers tend to dislike, such as gasoline or permanent markers. They may constantly sniff odd items.

Olfactory Activities

Searching for Cinnamon

Description: It is always fun to get your little ones in the kitchen. This twist on cooking will develop their ability to discriminate among smells, expose them to a variety of scents, and help them to be more adventurous.

Materials:
- Spices with strong scents, like basil, oregano, chili pepper
- Cinnamon
- Applesauce (or any other food that would be good with cinnamon)
- Bowl
- Spoon
- Blindfold

Space: Small

Time: 5 minutes

Setup: Pour the applesauce into a bowl. Pull out a variety of spices; fresh are best. If they are in a jar or bottle, open the lid to make it easier for your child to get a whiff.

Directions:

Step 1: Ask your child to smell the cinnamon.
Step 2: Blindfold your child.
Step 3: Ask them to tell you when they smell the cinnamon. Hand the spices, one by one, to your child so they can bring them to their nose. Eventually, hand them the cinnamon.
Step 4: When they identify the cinnamon, remove the blindfold.
Step 5: They can add a pinch of cinnamon to their applesauce, stir, and enjoy.

Make it a little easier: Instead of using spices, use scents like floral scented candles or essential oils (don't add to the applesauce, of course).

Make it a little harder: Pick scents that are similar to cinnamon, like nutmeg.

Additional Skills: Proprioceptive, Gustatory

Essentially Smelly

Description: I am a big fan of working with essential oils. Last summer at Play 2 Progress camp, we made magic "smelly" potions, and it was a bigger hit than I could have imagined. The kids *loved* smelling each oil and deciding which ones to add to their spray. Essential oils can also be used in monster repellent. Tell your child that you got the recipe for this monster repellent from Grandma and you know it works. Spray the baddies away!

Materials:
- Essential oils of your choice (lavender is generally a good bet, but your child may prefer other scents)
- Glass spray bottle (I use a four-ounce size, but any size is fine)
- Distilled or filtered water

Space: Small

Time: 10–15 minutes

Setup: Put your materials on the table.

Directions:

Step 1: Let your little one explore the smell of each of the oils and pick the one that they would like to use, or they can combine a few.
Step 2: Put five to ten drops of essential oil in the spray bottle.
Step 3: Add four ounces of water.
Step 4: Shake well and spray. Spray under the bed at bedtime to keep the monsters away. If there are no monsters to repel, spray wherever the child likes—bed, pillow, or around the room.

Make it a little easier: If your little one struggles when presented with too many options, make it easy and give them two essential oils to choose from.

Make it a little harder: Add a blindfold. Can they guess what they are smelling?

Additional Skills: Fine Motor

Scented Rice Bins

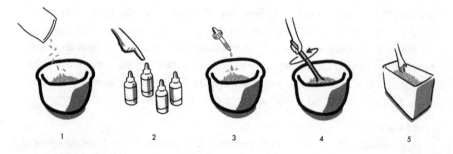

1   2   3   4   5

Description: This is a spin on those popular rice bins that you find all over Pinterest. It adds another sensory component to the tactile play, and kids can experiment with a spectrum of scents.

Materials:
- 4 to 6 cups of rice per bin
- Large bowl
- Essential oils (or natural scents, like fresh-squeezed lemon juice)
- Bin

Space: Small

Time: 10–15 minutes

Setup: Put all ingredients out on the table and you're ready to go.

Directions

Step 1: Pour the uncooked rice in a large bowl.

Step 2: Have your child choose a scent.

Step 3: Squeeze drops of essential oil into the rice. Start with ten or so, and work your way up to get the right amount. Twenty to twenty-five drops will be strong, so start slowly.

Step 4: Have your child mix the oil and the rice thoroughly using a spoon or their hands.

Step 5: Pour the dried rice into the bin and let them dig their hands in.

Make it a little easier: Make the scented rice for your little one after they have chosen the scent so all they have to do is play with the bin.

Make it a little harder: Can they guess the scent you used after you make the rice?

Additional Skills: Tactile

Guess Who?

Description: This is one for laundry day. It is also cool to see how well your little one can recognize family members solely by smell.

Materials:
- Shirts (previously worn, unlaundered) from all the members of the family
- Blindfold

Space: Small

Time: 5 minutes

Setup: Gather a pile of shirts from each member of your family.

Directions

Step 1: Blindfold your little one.
Step 2: Hand them one of the shirts.
Step 3: Ask them to smell the shirt and guess whose it is.
Step 4: Continue with the rest of the shirts.

Make it a little easier: Forget the blindfold.

Make it a little harder: Pick a few shirts from the same person to literally throw them off the scent.

Additional Skills: Proprioceptive

Lavender Sensory Sack

Description: Start with the scented rice recipe from page 158 to create a mini heating pad that is extra calming when your munchkin is sick or has a hard day.

Materials:
- 1 cup scented rice made with lavender oil (see page 158)
- 1 large clean sock
- Spoon
- Funnel (optional)
- Microwave

Space: Small

Time: 10 minutes

Setup: First make the scented rice with lavender oil (see page 158).

Directions

Step 1: Have your child fold down the top of the sock.

Step 2: They fill the sock two-thirds of the way with the scented rice.

Step 3: You tie the end securely.

Step 4: Microwave the sock for thirty seconds to one minute, checking how warm it is every fifteen seconds. Give it a shake to be sure there are no hot spots.

Step 5: Give it to your child to hold when they need some soothing.

Make it a little easier: Use a funnel to pour the rice into the sock rather than scooping.

Make it a little harder: Have your little one try to tie the end of the sock themselves.

Additional Skills: Fine Motor

Scented Playdough

Description: I do not enjoy the smell of the playdough you buy in stores. Here is an easy, all-natural version that will leave your little one's hands smelling sweet.

Materials:
- 1 cup flour
- ¼ cup salt
- 1 tablespoon cream of tartar
- 3 tablespoons canola oil
- 5 to 10 drops essential oil of your child's choice
- ¾ cup boiling water
- Small bowls or cups for holding each of the ingredients
- Mixing bowl

Space: Small

Time: 15–20 minutes

Setup: Pre-measure all the ingredients and place them on the table.

Directions

Step 1: Help your child mix the flour, salt, and cream of tartar in the mixing bowl until well combined.

Step 2: Next, have them add the canola oil and combine.

Step 3: You add the boiling water and essential oils and mix well (this step is for the adults).

Step 4: Once the dough has cooled down, knead it with your hands until it is no longer sticky. Add more flour if you need to, just like making bread.

Step 5: Once the playdough is ready, your little artist can start creating.

Make it a little easier: Help your little one knead the dough, or pre-make the playdough for them.

Make it a little harder: Don't pre-measure the ingredients; instead, have your child do all the measuring.

Additional Skills: Proprioceptive

Additional Olfactory Activities

Just by exploring their environment and going out to restaurants and friends' houses, your little one will be exposed to different smells, but here are a few activities that I recommend as well.

Board and other games
- Scented markers
- Cooking with you in the kitchen
- Scratch-and-sniff books and stickers
- Scented stuffed animals and dolls
- Essential oil smelling

SOUNDS GOOD!

Getting the Auditory System in Sync

. . . .

How many times have you been on the playground, in Mommy and Me class, or at a birthday party, heard a shriek for "MOMMMYYYYY" from across the room, and knew immediately that it was your little one? Because your auditory system is functioning correctly, you were able to distinguish that your child was in need and which direction to go running.

The auditory system, just like all our senses, is complex and has an impact on your child's overall capacity to stay regulated and their ability to learn at school. A well-functioning auditory system plays a key role in communication, too. It allows your child to hear a friend shout to them from across the playground and follow the instructions given by their teacher. Without a robust auditory system, a child has a difficult time playing Simon Says, learning the names of the classmates, and getting work done without being distracted by the noises made by classmates.

One of my first clients as an OT was this absolutely brilliant boy,

Jesse, who was imaginative, playful, and social but had difficulty with loud noises. He was one of the most popular kids in his class, and while I was working with him, he was invited to a birthday party at Disneyland with his classmates, which meant fireworks and a loud parade. Just the thought of it made Jesse retreat into a panic. At five years old, he had learned from Fourth of July celebrations, live shows, and birthday balloons popping unexpectedly that loud noises were not for him. Jesse's family was constantly on alert at parties and shows because if there was a sound he couldn't handle, they would be forced to leave the event and spend a half hour helping him calm his body. Because of his sensitivity, he missed out on a lot of activities, and it looked like he was going to miss this birthday party at Disney. We developed some strategies so he could tolerate loud noises as we continued to work on his sensitivity, like using noise-canceling earbuds when he knew there'd be fireworks (along with getting as far away as possible from the fireworks) so he could still attend.

A baby is able to hear their mother's voice in the womb. By the end of the pregnancy, they will be able to hear other voices as well, but their birth mom's will be the one that they prefer and respond to the most strongly. (I am always moved by the sight of a crying baby immediately calming at the sound of their parent's voice.) As they move into childhood, their auditory system develops further as they learn language, distinguish sounds, and continue to identify the soothing sounds of parents and caregivers.

As on OT, I often turn to speech therapists and audiologists who specialize in the auditory system for guidance. In the same way that vision is more than seeing 20/20, the auditory system is so much more than having good hearing. Your child needs to be able to process the noises that they hear, tune out background noises, discriminate between sounds, and tolerate a range of sounds and volumes. OTs also look at how children modulate auditory input: Do they jump at the slightest sound? Do they constantly have the volume on 11? We want to see if a child is under- or over-responsive to auditory input and how that impacts their daily life—Jesse, for example, was hugely over-responsive to that input.

We all have different tolerances to noise; I love listening to loud music, but I have friends who prefer the volume lower. Likewise, it is normal for your child to be annoyed by the vacuum or jump at a clap of thunder, but it should not impact their overall regulation. When it's having an impact on their learning or participation in events, or when they are constantly seeking out loud noises and unintentionally talking in a voice that is too loud for the situation, we know there might be an issue.

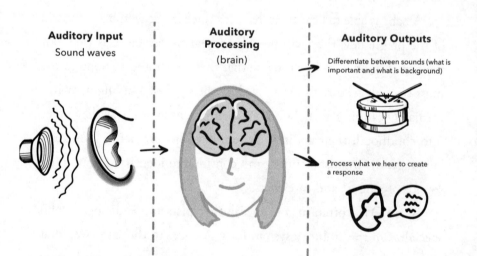

Auditory Input
Sound waves

Auditory Processing
(brain)

Auditory Outputs

Differentiate between sounds (what is important and what is background)

Process what we hear to create a response

The Auditory System

How the Auditory System Works

The ear is comprised of the outer ear, middle ear, and inner ear. The outer portion gathers the sound and sends it to the middle ear. The eardrum feels the vibrations generated by those sounds, which then progress to the inner ear, where they are converted into electrical signals and sent on to the brain for processing. That's when we create an output, or action, such as answering a question or following instructions. Auditory processing allows a child to discriminate between sounds ("pat" versus "bat"), distinguish between background noise and noise they need to pay attention to (critical in a classroom), remember what they hear (the names of their classmates), and sequence what they hear (following directions in order).

Key Aspects of Auditory Sense

Auditory discrimination: Once auditory input reaches the brain, it is processed to create a reaction, distinguish how loud something is (some kids are unaware of how loudly they are talking), sounds ("b" versus "d") and background noises, and remember what was heard and in what order.

Auditory modulation: Sometimes noises can feel too loud and completely dysregulate a child, or they might appear not to hear you (beyond just selectively ignoring you to get out of a chore). Another child might seek out more noise than others. A flushing toilet may be overwhelming for one child and can send them into tears, while their classmate will love the loud sound of a drum—and may seek to recreate it by pounding on a table.

Auditory Activities

. . . .

Dance . . . and Freeze

Description: This is a game the whole family can play. It will help your child distinguish among similar sounds while filtering out extraneous ones, which is a necessary skill for focusing in a classroom filled with their chatty peers.

Materials:
- Musical instruments (kids' instruments will do, or you can use pots and pans)
- Music

Space: Medium

Time: 5–15 minutes

Setup: Place musical instruments behind or under another object so your child cannot see which instrument you reach for.

Directions
. . . .

Step 1: Play your child's favorite music softly.

Step 2: Choose a "freeze" sound and let them hear it once or twice (i.e., strum a ukulele chord or hit a bongo) before you begin. Don't let them see the instrument.

Step 3: Dance party! Have your child stay within earshot of the music and instruments.

Step 4: Play the instruments one by one until you make the "freeze" sound. Make sure your child can't see the instrument itself, and be sure to keep the background music going.

Step 5: When your child hears the sound, they must freeze in place for ten seconds.

Step 6: Repeat steps 1–5, choosing a new "freeze" sound.

Make it a little easier: Don't play background music so the only noises are coming from the instruments, and have your little one move around the room until they hear the "freeze" sound.

Make it a little harder: Turn up the background music and have a true dance party.

Baby Bonus Activity: Let them explore the sounds of the different instruments.

Additional Skills: Vestibular, Proprioception

Chalking It Up

Description: Make your very own sidewalk chalk while working on sequencing.

Materials:
- Squeeze bottle (an old shampoo bottle will work)
- Cornstarch
- Water
- 5 drops food coloring (optional)
- Funnel (optional but helpful)

Space: Medium

Time: 5–15 minutes

Setup: Place all ingredients on the table. This recipe uses equal parts cornstarch and water. I suggest putting the exact amount of each ingredient you need in separate cups so your little one can easily pour them into the squeeze bottle.

Directions

Step 1: Give your child the directions in order before they begin. Tell them to first pour the cornstarch in the bottle, then pour in the water, then add the food coloring (if using), then put the lid on and shake.

Step 2: Let your little one try to sequence it alone. They need to follow all the steps you mentioned in the correct order, without your help.

Step 3: If they need a clue, repeat the entire sentence. You might want to simplify the sentence by just saying: "Cornstarch, water, food coloring, lid, and shake" if they are having trouble.

Step 4: Once everything is mixed, squirt it on the sidewalk to create a picture.

Make it a little easier: Have them carry out the directions two steps at a time, rather than doing all four in succession.

Make it a little harder: Don't repeat the sentence for them.

Additional Skills: Fine Motor

Copycat

Description: This classic game of telephone is great for a little one who is struggling with keeping their voice at an appropriate level to be more conscious of how loud they are speaking. It encourages them to lower their voice to pass the message along without the copycat hearing.

Materials:
- No materials, but you need at least three people (adults will do): a leader, a follower or followers, and a copycat.

Space: Medium

Time: 5–15 minutes

Setup: Have one person be the copycat. The copycat is going to try to hear what the leader is telling the other person, but the leader has to whisper so the copycat can't hear. Everyone stands in a circle with the copycat in the middle.

Directions

Step 1: The leader comes up with an action to tell the followers, e.g., "Do three jumping jacks" or "Find something red."

Step 2: The leader whispers the command to the followers.

Step 3: The copycat tries to hear what the leader is saying.

Step 4: After the leader has passed the message along, count to three. On three, everyone does the command. Did the copycat hear, or did they need to copy the task? If the copycat heard and successfully does the task, then the copycat wins.

Step 5: Switch places so everyone gets a turn at being the copycat.

Make it a little easier: Make the copycat stand farther away.

Make it a little harder: Add in more people, and it will be especially hard for the original message to make its way around.

Additional Skills: Praxis

Homemade Instruments

1   2+3+4   1   2   3

Description: Music is an amazing way to engage the auditory system, and it's even better if the instruments are homemade.

Materials:
- Empty bottles (glass is best)
- Water
- Rubber bands
- Empty shoe box or small box
- Chopstick
- Paper towel roll
- Glue

Space: Small

Time: 20–30 minutes

Setup: Put the materials out. You will make two instruments.

Directions: Musical Bottles

Step 1: You or your child pours various amounts of water into the bottles.

Step 2: If you have glass bottles, have your child use the chopstick to tap on the side of the glass to make music. If you are using a plastic container like an empty water bottle, they can blow into the top like a flute (you may have to show them how to do this).

Step 3: Listen to how the sound changes based on the level of water in the bottle.

Step 4: Can they make a xylophone? Can they arrange the bottles from low pitch to high pitch?

Directions: Rubber-Band Guitar

Step 1: Your child wraps four rubber bands around the open shoe box.

Step 2: Then they glue the paper towel roll to the top of the box.

Step 3: They just made a guitar! Time to rock.

Make it a little easier: Make one or all of the instruments for your little one and let them play.

Make it a little harder: Can they make a song with the instruments?

Baby Bonus Activity: Put the homemade guitar on the ground and let your babe rock out.

Additional Skills: Fine Motor, Tactile

Clap, Snap, Stomp

Description: There is nothing better than summer camp, and my years as a counselor are what launched my love for working with children. We played this activity whenever we had some time to burn. Little did I know that I would be playing it for years to come.

Materials:
- None

Space: Small

Time: 5–10 minutes

Setup: None

Directions

Step 1: Stand back-to-back with your little one.

Step 2: Come up with a sequence of claps, snaps, and stomps that they have to copy. Start easy with clap, clap, clap and move to more difficult sequences, but stick to using three sounds: clap, snap, and stomp.

Step 3: Now ask your child to repeat the sequence.

Step 4: Their turn! Can they come up with a new sequence for you to copy?

Step 5: Take turns coming up with combinations of claps, snaps, and stomps.

Make it a little easier: Play face-to-face instead of back-to-back.

Make it a little harder: Can they build on the sequence? After you start with clap, clap, clap, maybe they can add stomp, clap. You pick up the pattern with clap, clap, clap, stomp, clap and add more sounds. See how long you can each repeat the sequence.

Additional Skills: Praxis, Proprioception

Pat the Bat; Bat the Pat

Description: This is a goofy way to work on a hard concept. As someone who struggles with my auditory system, this activity can be challenging, so keep it light.

Materials:
• None

Space: Small

Time: 5–10 minutes

Setup: None

Directions

Step 1: Tell your little one to clap or stomp whenever they hear the word "pat."

Step 2: Now, say "pat" and "bat" in various combinations, and pause to make sure that they understand the directions and they clap when they hear "pat." Here are three sample sequences:

Easier: Bat, bat, bat, bat, bat (pause) pat (pause) bat, bat
Harder: Bat, pat, pat, bat, pat, bat, bat, bat, pat
Even harder: Pat, bat, pat, bat, bat, pat, bat, pat, pat, pat, bat, pat, bat

---

Make it a little easier: Pause for a second between each word.

Make it a little harder: Go faster (it is a serious tongue twister for you, too) and see how quickly they recognize the word you have asked them to listen for.

Additional Skills: Proprioception

Sounds Good

Description: See if your little one can follow the sound to find the music box.

Materials:
- Small music box (if you don't have a music box, a small portable speaker will do just fine)

Space: Medium

Time: 5–10 minutes

Setup: Start the music box playing and hide it.

Directions

Step 1: Tell your little one that you need their help to locate the music box.

Step 2: Send your little one off to find it.

Step 3: Once they've found it, hide the music box in a new spot and repeat.

Make it a little easier: Put the music box in an easy-to-find spot.

Make it a little harder: Hide the music box in something like the couch, where the sound may be muffled. Can they still hear and locate it?

Baby Bonus Activity: Hide a music box under a blanket and see if they can find it.

Additional Skills: Visual

Name That Song

Description: Break this out on family game night—everyone from kids to grandparents will have a blast. My preference is for classic Disney songs, but you can customize it with your little one's best-loved music.

Materials:
- A device to play music

Space: Small

Time: 5–10 minutes

Setup: Get an instrumental playlist, or develop your own, of songs that they know.

Directions

Step 1: Tell your child that they need to guess the song.

Step 2: Press play and let them guess. Once they guess it they need to write it down (or draw it if they can't write yet) and put their thumb up. You can pick anything from Raffi to Disney, but it should be a song that they will recognize even without the words.

Step 3: Once everyone has finished, show your paper and see who guessed right.

Step 4: Repeat with a new song.

Make it a little easier: Use the song with the lyrics.

Make it a little harder: Add a time limit for how long they have to guess.

Additional Skills: Fine Motor

Additional Auditory Activities

Many common childhood games require careful listening or following instructions. The following are some of my picks.

Backyard/outdoor/indoor games
- Simon Says
- Asking your little one to get you something, e.g., "Bring me a red-and-blue beanbag or your shoes, coat, and shirt."
- Playing musical chairs
- Freeze dancing
- Playing with instruments
- Creating a song
- Clapping on a beat
- Going to a park and naming the sounds you hear
- Playing telephone
- Red Rover

Board games
- Hullabaloo

THE SENSE INSIDE THE BODY

Being Aware of Interoception

. . . .

This final sense is truly the most hidden one of all—in fact, you may not have heard of it. It is called interoception, and it is our internal sense of our body. It helps us identify if we are hot, cold, hungry, thirsty, or need to go to the bathroom. It also plays a role in interpreting what we are feeling based on sensations in our body. As you can imagine, this sense is vital to our overall regulation. Kelly Mahler, an OT who has studied interoception and wrote *The Interoception Curriculum: A Step-by-Step Framework for Developing Mindful Self-Regulation*, says that it answers the question "How do I feel?" The next step, once we recognize the feeling, is acting on it to get the body back in balance. Feeling hungry leads to eating.

One example that illustrates the function and influence of interoception is potty training, which happens around age three (but every child is different). The first step to potty training is for your kid to be able to identify that they have to go to the bathroom. The interoceptive sense helps us determine that need, so you can imagine the difficulty a toddler will experience if they can't feel in their body that they have to go to the bathroom. Delays in potty training can be frustrating for both parents and children, particularly when there may be a push to complete it before the child can enroll in daycare or school.

Interoception also lets us know when we are hungry or thirsty. When your child's tummy is rumbling, they know to get a snack or ask for one, and then to stop eating when they are full. When they have been running around the playground on a warm day, interoception gives them the sense that they are thirsty and to seek out a cool drink.

Additionally, interoception is responsible for how we understand the emotions we experience in our bodies. Your child may feel their heart beating faster if they hear a creak that they are convinced is a closet monster or something lurking under the bed. They will identify their heart thumping with that fear, but it will ideally also guide them to turn on the night-light so that they feel safe. If a child has a good sense of interoception, they will feel these kinds of emotions—linked to their physical sensations—more deeply. Interoception is essential for emotional regulation. A child needs to notice internal cues and identify what they mean so that they can run to the potty or grab a snack before they get into meltdown territory. As children are learning to read their internal cues, parents and caregivers can encourage them to make the connection: "I see that you are moving your body; I wonder if you need to go to the bathroom?"

As I learn more about interoception, I think of my own journey to improve this sense. I've progressed from a child who, according to my mom, "would never potty train," to an adult with an autoimmune disease who had to learn to be acutely aware of my body cues to stay healthy and protect myself. I also used to snap and quickly devolve into tantrums. I couldn't recognize how and where my emotions were manifesting until my cup was overflowing. It wasn't until adulthood that I found mindfulness, which gave me the ability to identify where I felt those emotions and assess my overall internal state. These days, I can feel when I am getting anxious and know when I need to pull back. I can also feel when my body is becoming inflamed and turn to the foods that nourish me and make sure to rest.

We want to teach children to recognize the information their body is sending them about their emotions and feelings. Parents can be supportive by using specific language (e.g., "Wow, I can see you are feeling a big emotion. I noticed you threw your cup. Your body bucket must feel really full."). Particularly when it comes to emotions, if a child can identify the first sign of upset in their bodies, then they can draw on what we OTs often refer to as a toolbox to calm down.

REGULATION TOOLS

- Establish a calming corner, like a tent or a nook area with no stimulation. This isn't a space for a time-out, but rather a soothing spot with weighted stuffed animals, one or two books, and some pillows. (See page 111.)
- Have a set of tools that your child can access at school or at home, like a bin containing calming items such as a squish ball, fidgets, a small weighted ball, and resistance bands. (See page 55.)
- Create a glitter jar (see page 187) for support during dysregulation.
- Provide them with a few soothing essential oils that they can smell to help them breathe and calm down.

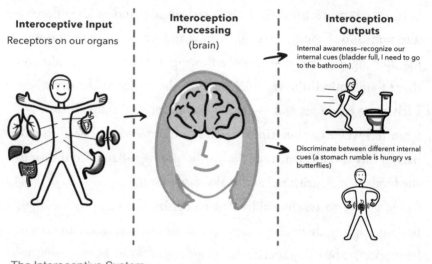

Interoceptive Input	Interoception Processing	Interoception Outputs
Receptors on our organs	(brain)	Internal awareness–recognize our internal cues (bladder full, I need to go to the bathroom)
		Discriminate between different internal cues (a stomach rumble is hungry vs butterflies)

The Interoceptive System

How the Interoceptive System Works

Our organs hold many interoceptive receptors. The signals created by these receptors are sent to the areas of our brain that handle homeostasis—our ability to stay regulated and function well. Interoception is complex—more complex than our other senses. (In fact, there is debate about whether to categorize it as its own sense, but for the sake of this book, we will refer to it as the eighth sense.)

You may have heard the term "interoceptive awareness," which refers to our ability to recognize internal cues (e.g., belly full, feeling tired) in order to identify a feeling and act on it to stay regulated or in homeostasis. There isn't much research on the development of interoceptive awareness in infants, but one study has shown that some babies are more sensitive than others to their interoceptive cues (in this case, by using their heartbeats). Recent studies have also examined how interoception and specifically interoceptive awareness play a role in anxiety, autism, ADHD, and other emotional or behavioral disorders. Understanding their internal cues helps your child to be socially aware, regulated, and intuitive—which are all foundations for academic and social success.

Key Aspects of Interoception

Interoceptive discrimination: It is important to be able to discriminate between internal cues—for example, a stomach grumble of hunger is different from nausea. Identifying the feeling and being able to act accordingly will help your kiddo feel right in their body. Some kids may have trouble understanding what their body is telling them and exactly where the sensation is coming from, causing anxiety and difficulty staying regulated. A child may feel butterflies out of excitement but mistake the feeling for fear and get nervous about going to that sleepover.

Interoceptive modulation: Just like the other seven senses, while we look for the just-right response to interoceptive inputs, a child may over- or under-respond to the messages they receive about feelings or emotions. A little one might not feel that they need to go to the bathroom until the very last minute or they may be extra sensitive and run for the potty before they may actually need to go.

Interoception Activities

Where Do I Feel That in My Body?

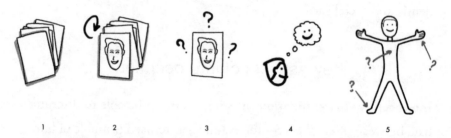

| 1 | 2 | 3 | 4 | 5 |

Description: This mindfulness activity will guide your child to recognize how and where their emotions resonate in their body.

Materials:
- Printed-out pictures of faces expressing distinct emotions (I like using actual pictures of the child)
- Glue
- Heavy paper or cardstock

Space: Small

Time: 10–15 minutes

Setup: Cut out the faces and make each into an individual card by gluing them to heavy paper or cardstock.

Directions

Step 1: Place the images facedown on a table or stack them up.

Step 2: Your child selects a card, turns it over, and looks at the image.

Step 3: Ask them to identify what emotion is on the face.

Step 4: Ask them to tell you about a time when they felt that emotion.

Step 5: Ask them to point out where on their body they feel that feeling. If they need help, give them examples: "Sometimes I feel fear in my heart when it beats." Or, "When I am excited, I feel it in my arms and legs, and I want to jump up and down."

Step 6: Repeat steps 1–5 until all the cards have been used.

Be sure to keep the game child-centered and give your kid time for thinking and answering. They may not be aware of how their body feels, even if you are. Keep in mind that their body may feel different from yours, too.

Make it a little easier: If they are having trouble making a connection between a card and an emotion they have experienced, you can give them some assistance. For example: "I remember you were so excited when we were on our way to Disneyland."

Make it a little harder: Use more abstract emotions, like "bored."

Additional Skills: Proprioception

Balloon Boom

Description: This is an easy activity to show your little one how to feel their own heartbeat and point out how their heart rate increases when they are surprised or scared.

Materials:
- Balloon
- Something to pop the balloon (I use a paper clip)

Space: Small

Time: 5–10 minutes

Setup: Blow up the balloon.

Directions

Step 1: Tell your little one that you are going to pop the balloon and then the two of you are going to explore how their heart feels after the pop.

Step 2: Ask them to come up with a prediction. What do they think their heart will feel like after the pop?

Step 3: Do not tell them when you are going to pop the balloon. Make sure you are close enough that the sound will be loud, but they can't see your hands so it is a surprise.

Step 4: Pop that balloon.

Step 5: Have them put their hands on their heart and see if it is beating faster.

Step 6: Talk about how, when we are scared or surprised, our hearts beat faster.

Make it a little easier: If your little one struggles with surprises, have them pop the balloon.

Make it a little harder: Turn off the lights. Do the activity in the dark.

Additional Skills: Auditory

Glitter Jar

Description: This is an easy-to-use tool that helps children get through hard moments by giving them a chance to pause and breathe. Glitter jars are extremely effective, and kids take to them quickly (one of my kiddos even handed hers to her dad when he was upset with her).

Materials:
- Mason jar
- 1 cup water
- ¼ cup glue
- ½ cup glitter of their choice

Space: Small

Time: 5–10 minutes

Setup: Place all the materials on the table.

Directions

Step 1: Have your child pour water into the mason jar.

Step 2: Then, they will add the glue.

Step 3: Glitter goes in next.

Step 4: Put the lid on the mason jar, making sure it is well sealed, and shake it until all ingredients are well combined. If you want a better seal, you can hot-glue the inside edge of the lid before screwing it onto the jar.

Step 5: Explain to your little one that when you shake the jar, it is just like our mind, with lots of thoughts and feelings moving fast. Tell them that they can calm their mind by watching and breathing as the glitter slowly settles at the bottom of the jar.

Step 6: Remind your child to use this tool when they are upset so they can pause, take a breath, and then talk it out.

Make it a little easier: Make the jar for them.

Make it a little harder: Add a particular type of glitter for various feelings (e.g., stars for anger or purple for sad).

Additional Skills: Fine Motor

Additional Interoceptive Activities

These activities can help your child to connect with what is going on inside their bodies.

Backyard/outdoor/indoor games
- Yoga
- Breathing activities
- Kelly Mahler's Body Check Chart

Books
- *Listening to My Body* by Gabi Garcia
- *Peaceful Piggy Meditation* by Kerry Lee MacLean

Meditation apps
- Insight Timer for kids
- Headspace for kids
- Calm
- Moshi

10

MAKING A PLAN

Praxis in Action

. . . .

Now that you know about all eight senses, it is time to teach you another concept: praxis. You may not be familiar with the word "praxis," but you have definitely seen it in action. In fact, we use praxis every day. It's a skill that your child can develop as they are exposed to different situations and physical challenges. In *Sensory Integration and the Child*, Jean Ayres defines praxis as the ability to conceptualize, plan, and sequence a new activity. When you bring your child to a park with a giant play structure, they have to plan how they are going to get over to it, carry out the movements they will need to get to the top, and then do it.

As you can imagine, praxis has a massive influence on a child's self-esteem and sense of belonging. I often think of how my own sense of praxis had an impact on my self-confidence during my teenage years. I have never been the most coordinated person, but because of how hard I try, I can generally keep up. After cheerleading from third grade through high school, I got cut from the team my senior year, which crushed me. I lost much of my self-confidence, and it wasn't until years later, when I was in OT school, began practicing yoga, and learned about the sensory system that I was able to understand it all. We don't want kids to experience rejection or a lack of self-confidence when there are so many ways we can help them in their early years.

We break down praxis into smaller components so a child can master each aspect. First, a child needs to use ideation (thinking about what they want to do). Then they need to motor plan and sequence (come up with the steps they are going to take and the order they will do them in) and finally execute their plan.

Let's break it down a bit more.

How Praxis Works

Ideation is the part of praxis that I see more and more kids struggling with as screens and toys that light up and move on their own become increasingly prevalent. Many electronic games follow a prescribed path or sequence of moves so playing with them becomes a passive, repetitive series of actions rather than drawing on a child's creativity to play or make progress in the game. Many toys also immediately direct a child toward *how* to play and the options are limited—e.g., an electric truck that goes only forward and back versus a bucket and some sticks, which provide open-ended entertainment. Open-ended toys—those that can be played with flexibility and ingenuity—are few and far between, and we have lost the art of using household items to stimulate a child's imagination. (This is why we created the Animagnets at Play 2 Progress.) In our online music and movement class, I ask the kids to run around their house and gather items that can be instruments. There's only one rule: it can't be an actual instrument. When I first introduced this game, I expected them to grab pots and pans and items that they could bang to make noise, but many of them struggle to find an item that would work; recently a child brought back a Barbie.

OPEN-ENDED TOYS

Open-ended toys are indispensable for imaginative play, adaptable to all sorts of games, and can transform in an instant. Pots and pans are a drum set; cups, hats are unicorn horns; a cardboard box is a racecar, spaceship, or home for stuffed animals. Instead of reaching for the battery-powered device, try offering your child:

- Pots and pans
- Crumpled paper
- Drawing paper
- Newspaper
- Animagnets
- Wood toys (like wood blocks)
- Cups
- Water
- Chalk
- Squirt bottles
- Empty boxes
- Any non-electronic household objects and toys

When your child wants to play, they first need to decide what they are going to do. For example, if they find a bucket in the backyard, are they going to fill it with water, drag it across the yard, and water the flowers, or are they going to turn it upside down, find a stick, and make it into a drum? This is ideation—the process of coming up with an idea to pursue.

Once your child formulates their idea, the next step is for them to plan and sequence their movements. If they have decided to fill the bucket with water, how are they going to do it? They may discover that if they tilt it, the water will spill out and they need to bring it closer to the hose. Or they may figure out that they can't fill the bucket to the top and get all the water to the flowers. If they make the bucket into a drum, how will they get the stick to be a drumstick? Will they walk on the path or through the flowers? They can call on this motor planning and exploration the next time they play in the yard. In fact, once they have been taught and practice the motor planning for a specific movement (e.g., tying shoes), most of the time they will remember and be able to repeat it. This comes in handy for sports, writing, and games.

The final step is executing the plan; this is when your child completes the action. They cross the yard, get the bucket, put the hose inside, fill it, and water the flowers. This also requires that they have the muscle strength and physical ability needed for the specific action. They may not be able to do it exactly as planned, but they may also compensate by emptying out some water if it is too heavy and making a few trips to the tap.

As you can imagine, the other senses impact praxis and motor planning. If a child has trouble with motor planning, they may have dyspraxia. A child who is dyspraxic (struggles with praxis) may be clumsy and have trouble with both fine and gross motor skills, which can impact their friendships and self-confidence. Kids with dyspraxia may also prefer to play sedentary and solitary games rather than active ones, which can lead to obesity and other consequences of an inactive lifestyle. Keep in mind, however, that much of motor planning involves trial and error. A child filling a bucket with water may spill a lot the first time, but they will do better with repetition and mastery, so you should encourage their efforts, even if it's frustrating to watch.

One of the best ways to promote praxis is by exploring and playing. Use what you have around the house, make forts, go on explorations in your yard, and encourage imaginative play.

Praxis Activities

The Floor Is Lava

1 + 2   3 + 4   5

Description: Long before the reality show came out, generations of kids played this game. Careful not to get burned!

Materials:

- Items your child can stand on (couch pillows, floor spots, yoga mats, stools, laundry baskets, and anything that will keep them from touching the "lava")

Space: Large

Time: 30+ minutes

Setup: Put all the items in one big pile.

Directions

Step 1: You and your child pick a starting point (e.g., the kitchen table).

Step 2: Next, pick an ending point (e.g., the living-room couch).

Step 3: Tell your little one the floor is about to turn into lava and they need to build a safe path to get from the starting point to the ending point that will keep them from touching the lava.

Step 4: Give them about thirty minutes, longer if they need it, to build the path. As they are building, if you notice something you know won't work, rather than telling them, ask them to test it out. You may need to assist for safety.

Step 5: Once they have built the course, tell them the lava has been released, and it's time for them to follow their path to the finish line.

Make it a little easier: Build the obstacle course and have them follow the path from beginning to end.

Make it a little harder: Add a time limit, give them a set number of items they can use (e.g., one cushion, the laundry basket, and two chairs), identify specific items they have to use (the blue laundry basket, the yellow pillow), or have them collect items throughout the house themselves.

Baby Bonus Activity: Set up a baby-friendly obstacle course. Put their favorite toy on the other side of some couch pillows and watch them figure out how to climb over.

Additional Skills: Proprioception

Kitchen Rock Band

Description: Anyone can form a band, no instruments required. Make drums out of pots and pans and work on that first critical step of praxis: ideation.

Materials:
- Household items (pots and pans, Tupperware, cups, blocks, wooden spoons)

Space: Small

Time: 20–30 minutes

Setup: No setup necessary.

Directions

Step 1: It is time to create a kitchen rock band, but because kitchen rock bands don't use traditional instruments, tell your little one that they have to make their own. Have them go around the house (or the room you are in) and find something to transform into an instrument.

Step 2: Try not to guide them to a choice—let them explore how items work together to generate a sound.

Step 3: Once your child has found their instrument, it is time to rock out.

Step 4: Can they make another instrument? Can they make an instrument so you can jam along?

Make it a little easier: Put a few items out that your little one can use to make an instrument to get the process started.

Make it a little harder: Add a time limit and tell them they can use only items found in a specific room.

Baby Bonus Activity: Let them explore container play and making noise with pots and pans.

Additional Skills: Auditory

What Could It Be?

Description: This form of imaginary play can be done with anything, anywhere, and brings me back to my days rocking out to Hanson using a hairbrush as my microphone (don't judge). It is another excellent activity for practicing ideation.

Materials:
- Literally any item you can hold. What is in your hand right now—this book? Great! That works! You could also use a fork, or a plastic container, or a spoon. Anything goes.
- Timer

Space: Small

Time: 5–10 minutes

Setup: None needed

Directions

Step 1: Hand your little one three items and ask them how many things these three items can be. They can use their body and any other props that are in the area. You may want to give them an example, like, "This bowl could be a hat."

Step 2: Start a one-minute timer and let them come up with as many uses as they can. Is that cup a phone? A unicorn horn? What else?

Step 3: Repeat with more items.

Make it a little easier: Forget the timer.

Make it a little harder: Pick items that are a bit trickier to come up with an alternate use, like a hairbrush or a piece of paper.

Baby Bonus Activity: Give them materials like crumpled paper, plastic cups, etc., and let them play and explore.

Additional Skills: Proprioception

Wicked Web

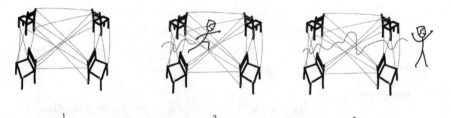

1   2   3

Description: If you were to walk into Play 2 Progress on any day, you might see string all over one of our small rooms and a few intrepid kiddos trying to maneuver from one side to the other without getting tangled up.

Materials:
- A spool of yarn or string
- Four sturdy chairs

Space: Large

Time: 30+ minutes

Setup: Make a square out of the four chairs with about two to three feet between each one. Now take the yarn and string it in multiple directions, creating a spider web between the chairs.

Directions

Step 1: It is time for your little one to turn into a creepy-crawly spider. Give them the challenge of getting through the yarn web from one side to the other without getting caught.

Step 2: Watch as they step over, crawl under, and go sideways through the web. Sometimes they will get caught as they motor plan their way through. Allow them to figure out how to get untangled.

Step 3: Celebrate if they make it through without getting caught.

Make it a little easier: Make a simple web.

Make it a little harder: Can your child make the web before navigating it?

Additional Skills: Proprioception

A-Mazing!

1   2   3

Description: A corn maze—without the corn.

Materials:
- Painters' tape
- Bucket
- Beanbags

Space: Large

Time: 15–20 minutes

Setup: Create a maze on the floor using painters' tape. Place a bucket at one end of the maze and a beanbag at the start (or more than one, if they will repeat the activity).

Directions

Step 1: Challenge your little one to bring the beanbag to the bucket without stepping on the tape or hitting a dead end.

Step 2: Have them navigate through the maze to the bucket.

Step 3: Now can they make it back to get the rest of the beanbags?

Make it a little easier: Set up a simple maze.

Make it a little harder: Can they make the maze?

Additional Skills: Visual

Hula-Hoop Hustle

Description: It's fun to watch kids work out how to solve this problem. During your next game night, the whole family can see if they're up for the challenge.

Materials:

- Two Hula-Hoops (more if doing a race). I find the heavy, water-filled Hula-Hoops tend to be the best.

Space: Large

Time: 15–20 minutes

Setup: Pick starting and ending points, like opposite sides of the yard.

Directions

Step 1: Hand your child both Hula-Hoops.

Step 2: Their challenge is to get from the start to the end, but they can only step inside the Hula-Hoops, and they only get to use two hoops.

Step 3: Watch as they figure out what they need to do to complete the task. Resist telling them, and give them some time to work it out on their own:

Put down the two hoops,

step into the first hoop,

then step into the second hoop,

turn around and pick up the first hoop that is now behind them and move it in front.

They continue this process until they have made it to the end.

Make it a little easier: Show them how you do it using two floor spots.

Make it a little harder: Make it a race. Who can get to the other side first?

Additional Skills: Proprioception

Keep It Up

1   2   3

Description: This is a twist on the classic game "Keep Up the Balloon." The chalk circles add a challenge that helps your child work on their motor planning.

Materials:
- An inflated balloon
- Chalk (you can use floor spots or pillows if you are playing inside)

Space: Large

Time: 25–30 minutes

Setup: Draw six to eight large circles a few inches apart on the driveway.

Directions

Step 1: Your kid can't let the balloon touch the ground, and they can only step in the circles as they keep it up without holding it.

Step 2: Throw the balloon to them. Remind them that they cannot hold the balloon, so they should keep hitting it.

Step 3: How long can they keep the balloon up?

Make it a little easier: Put the circles closer together.

Make it a little harder: Spread the circles out.

Additional Skills: Visual, Proprioception, Vestibular

Additional Praxis Activities

Free play can get your child planning and moving—try some of these!

Backyard/outdoor games
- Visiting a new playground
- Rock climbing
- Yoga
- Sports

Board and other games
- Open-ended toys—wooden blocks, simple stuffed animals, anything without batteries
- Playing with household items
- Using cardboard boxes or toilet paper rolls to create structures, sculptures
- Twister
- Heads Up
- River Stones
- Yeti in My Spaghetti
- Cat in the Hat I Can Do That!
- Charades

11

POWER AT THE FINGERTIPS

Building Fine Motor Skills

. . . .

Now, I want to jump into a topic that I get asked about daily: activities to work on a child's fine motor skills, which use the tiny muscles in the hands and fingers. Of course, our sensory system influences our fine motor skills, and without a solid basis in all the senses, they can be an issue. Thus far, we have been talking primarily about our eight senses—using muscles and arms and legs to do things like walk, jump, or climb. Fine motor skills influence the precision of movements like buttoning a button or holding a paintbrush or pencil correctly. Children use them every day to get dressed, eat, make crafts, write, cut, tie their shoes, and do their hair (I mention the last one because when children with long hair struggle with hair ties, it can be frustrating). I could write an entire book on this topic, as there is so much that goes into fine motor skills, and the root to our fine motor skills is a strong sensory system, but for our purposes, here are the basics.

Fine motor skills begin to develop in the first year of life. Your infant reaching for a toy is the start of developing their fine motor ability, and picking up a piece of cereal with their pointer and thumb is another step.

I will mention here that we also need to be able to cross the midline of the body—a right-handed child who is able to draw on the far left-hand side of their paper is crossing the midline. The majority of children have an innate dominant hand, which is normal and even essential to skill development; however, they should be able to use their dominant hand with ease on both sides of their body. When a child switches between hands—rather than having one clear dominant hand—it is often not a sign that they are ambidextrous but actually an indication that they are not fluidly crossing their midline.

Other aspects of fine motor development include:

- In-hand manipulation: This is the ability to shift small items within one hand without using the other. If a child has a handful of pennies that they want to place into their piggy bank, they will be able to move the pennies from their palm to their fingertips and then drop them in using fine motor skills. It also means they can readjust their grasp on a pencil to move their hand closer to the lead, spin the pencil in their fingers, or flip it to use the eraser.
- Grasp: Grasp is more than how your child holds utensils or a pencil. It progresses from grasping and shaking a rattle all the way to holding and writing with a pencil, with many grasp patterns in between. Examples include picking up Cheerios, blocks, and chunky toddler crayons. I am not a stickler about a child having a proper grip (I certainly don't have one), but I look to see if they are able to complete all their daily tasks neatly and efficiently with endurance. If a client's grasp is not

technically perfect but their handwriting is good and they can write for a period of time without tiring, then I don't worry about how exactly they hold the pencil.

- Bilateral coordination: This is the ability to use both hands together to complete a task. When a child is cutting out a circle from a larger piece of paper, they need to use their power (dominant) hand to use the scissors and their helper (non-dominant) hand to hold and rotate it.

Before you sit at the table to practice fine motor skills, make sure that your little one is in a good postural position, otherwise it will be much more difficult for them to be stable in their body and to use their hands. On that note, if they are an extra sloppy eater, check their sitting position and see if adjusting it helps them control their utensils.

PROPER POSTURAL POSITION

Positioning tips:

- **Have them sit in a stable chair that has a back.**
- **Scoot their tush all the way to the back of the chair so that their torso is flush to the seat back.** If they can't do this with their feet touching the floor, put a few firm pillows behind them until their feet are flat on the floor. If their feet still can't reach a hard surface, use a footstool.
- **Scoot their chair into the table.**

Fine Motor Skills Activities

Egg Carton Color Matching

1   2   3

Description: This one is simple but fun. Grab the supplies from your kitchen and start playing.

Materials:
- Mini tongs
- Colored pom-poms or painted/colored cotton balls
- Empty egg carton or muffin tin
- Markers or paint that match the colors of the pom-poms

Space: Small

Time: 15–20 minutes

Setup: Color or paint the inside bottom of the egg cartons or muffin tin. If you don't want to paint the tin, paint or color the inside bottom of cupcake liners and insert them into your tin. Each section should be a different color, matching the colors of your pom-poms.

Directions

Step 1: Give your child the mini tongs.
Step 2: Place the pile of pom-poms next to them.
Step 3: Have your child use the tongs to pick up each pom one by one and place it in the space of the egg carton or muffin tin with the matching color. Encourage them to find all the colors.

Make it a little easier: Have your child use their fingers instead of tongs to practice their pincer grasp.

Make it a little harder: Use chopsticks instead of tongs.

Baby Bonus Activity: If your little one isn't quite ready for the tongs, have them use their thumb and pointer finger to pick up the pom-poms and place them in the muffin tins and forget the color matching.

Additional Skills: Visual

Spongey Stamps

Description: This spin on stamps is an enjoyable way to get a child to practice writing their name.

Materials:
- Sponge
- Paint
- Paper
- Pencil
- Plate or paint tray

Space: Small

Time: 15–20 minutes

Setup: On a large piece of paper, write your child's name in big letters. Cut a kitchen sponge into small squares. Squirt some paint onto a plate.

Directions

Step 1: Have your child dip a sponge square into the paint.
Step 2: They then place a "stamp" of paint on part of the first letter of their name.
Step 3: They continue coloring the letters by stamping each until their name is completed.

Make it a little easier: Instead of coloring the letters of their name, make a few large shapes on the paper and ask your child to stamp inside each shape.

Make it a little harder: Have your child write their own name before stamping.

Baby Bonus Activity: Cut the sponge in half and let your little one stamp paint on a large piece of paper. Try putting the paper on the floor and letting them "paint" while in their diaper to fully explore the sponge, paint, and paper.

Additional Skills: Visual, Tactile

Pipe Cleaner and Strainer

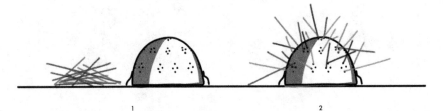

1   2

Description: This is an easy activity to pull out when you need to cook dinner while keeping your little one occupied.

Materials:
- Pipe cleaners
- Strainer

Space: Small

Time: 5–10 minutes

Setup: Put the materials on the table.

Directions

Step 1: Tell your child to flip the strainer upside down and place it on the table.

Step 2: Then, have them stick the pipe cleaners into the strainer holes.

Make it a little easier: Use an old strainer and cut some of the holes to make them larger.

Make it a little harder: Have them try to get the pipe cleaners into the strainer while blindfolded.

Baby Bonus Activity: Have your little one place cotton balls in a mason jar.

Additional Skills: Visual, Tactile

Clothes on a Line

1   2   3   4

Description: Any child who enjoys playing with dolls and taking care of their clothes goes nuts for this one. If your little one is not interested in doll clothes, they can hang up paper animals instead.

Materials:
- Doll clothes
- Paper animals (optional). Print out animals and cut them out. You can laminate if you want to use again.
- Clothespins
- Yarn
- Two chairs

Space: Medium

Time: 20–30 minutes

Setup: Tie the yarn to two chairs about four feet apart to create a clothes-line about the height of your child's chest.

Directions

Step 1: Have your child pick up a clothespin and a piece of clothing.
Step 2: They pin the clothes on the line.
Step 3: They continue pinning until all the clothes are hung up.
Step 4: Now, they can take all the clothes off the line and put them back where they belong.

Make it a little easier: You hang up the clothes, and the child pulls them off the line and puts them away.

Make it a little harder: Use mini clothespins.

Additional Skills: Proprioception, Visual

Q-Tip Handwriting

Description: Q-tips are a fantastic way to practice fine motor skills and work on grasp. Kids find it entertaining to paint with something other than brushes, too.

Materials:
- Q-tips
- Paint
- Paper (I like large handwriting paper with solid lines/dotted lines and recommend Handwriting Without Tears)
- Paint tray

Space: Small

Time: 25–30 minutes

Setup: Pour the paint onto the paint tray and place all materials on the table.

Directions:

Step 1: Tell your child to pick up the Q-tip and dip the end of it into the paint.

Step 2: Have them practice writing their name or drawing shapes using the Q-tip as a brush.

Make it a little easier: Instead of writing their name, have them trace letters and shapes that you write on the paper.

Make it a little harder: Draw an infinity symbol on the paper and have them trace it with paint on the Q-tip.

Additional Skills: Tactile, Visual

Silly Stickers

1   2   3

Description: All kids love finding stickers in the junk drawer and decorating everything with them (even the walls), so why not use that affinity to work on fine motor skills?

Materials:
- Small colored circular stickers, or any stickers you have around
- Paper
- Markers

Space: Small

Time: 20–25 minutes

Setup: Draw the trunk of a tree and the branches. Draw small circles that are slightly bigger than the twigs coming off the branches.

Directions:

Step 1: Give your child the drawing you made.
Step 2: Ask them to give the tree leaves by peeling a sticker and placing it inside the circles on the branches.
Step 3: They keep going until all the circles are covered in stickers and you have a colorful fall tree.

Make it a little easier: Leave out the circles and let them place the stickers wherever they want to fill up the tree.

Make it a little harder: Ask your child to draw the tree.

Additional Skills: Visual, Tactile

Jumping, Shaking Beans

Description: Activate your child's imagination with a homemade instrument.

Materials:
- Funnel
- Empty water bottle
- Uncooked beans
- Bowl
- Spoon

Space: Small

Time: 10–15 minutes

Setup: Place the funnel inside the water bottle and pour the beans in the bowl.

Directions

Step 1: Your child scoops beans into the funnel using the spoon.

Step 2: Once the water bottle is about one-third filled with beans, put the lid on and twist it closed.

Step 3: They can shake their homemade maraca around. You could even put on music to accompany them.

Make it a little easier: Use a sand shovel or a soup ladle instead of a spoon to scoop the beans into the funnel.

Make it a little harder: Ditch the funnel and carefully spoon the beans directly into the water bottle.

Additional Skills: Visual, Tactile

Uh-Oh Cheerios

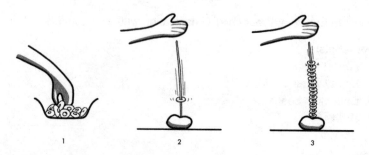

Description: Cheerios provide a natural way to work on fine motor skills starting at a young age, and they make edible beads as well.

Materials:
- Playdough
- Cheerios
- Raw spaghetti
- Bowl

Space: Small

Time: 15–20 minutes

Setup: Roll the playdough into a ball and stick it onto the table. Stick four spaghetti noodles into the playdough so they are standing straight up. Pour out a small bowl of Cheerios.

Directions

Step 1: Your child picks up a Cheerio.
Step 2: They carefully place it on a spaghetti noodle.
Step 3: Complete until the bowl is empty and there is a stack of Cheerios on each noodle.

Make it a little easier: Use large beads and pipe cleaners instead of Cheerios and spaghetti.

Make it a little harder: Have your child do the setup. Can they place the spaghetti into the playdough without it breaking? What about the Cheerios? Can they pour without spilling?

Additional Skills: Visual, Proprioception, Tactile

Crumpled Paper Stamps

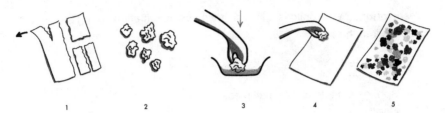

Description: Making stamps, rather than using store-bought ones, by grabbing what is available at home allows kids to use their creativity—and incorporates many fine motor skills.

Materials:
- Paper
- Paint
- Paint tray

Space: Small

Time: 20–25 minutes

Setup: Pour the paint onto the paint tray.

Directions

Step 1: Your child rips the paper into different-size pieces.

Step 2: They crumple the paper into small balls.

Step 3: They dip the crumpled ball into the paint.

Step 4: They use the paper "stamp" to create a textured painting.

Step 5: They continue with different colors and different-size balls to produce a cool abstract design.

Make it a little easier: Rip the paper for your child.

Make it a little harder: Draw a few shapes for them to stamp inside. This will give them practice staying inside the lines.

Additional Skills: Tactile

Goin' Fishin'

Description: If your child is a little fish who loves bath time, bring fine motor practice into the tub.

Materials:
- Large spoon
- Sponge cut into eight small pieces
- Cup

Space: Small

Time: 15–20 minutes

Setup: Dump the sponge pieces into the bath.

Directions

Step 1: Give your child the cup and spoon.
Step 2: Ask them to catch the "fishies" (sponge pieces) by scooping them up with the spoon and putting them in the cup.

Make it a little easier: Use a cup to scoop the fish instead of a spoon.

Make it a little harder: Use tongs instead of a spoon.

Additional Skills: Visual, Tactile

Additional Fine Motor Skills Activities

Working on fine motor skills can be done with supplies you likely have around the house.

Outdoor/indoor games
- Chalk on the sidewalk or driveway
- Crayons/markers and paper for coloring
- Coloring books
- Cooking
- Cutting playdough using either playdough scissors or kid-friendly scissors
- Beads
- Eating with utensils
- Playing with pretend tools
- Painting
- Molding and building shapes with playdough
- Using shovels and buckets

Board and other games
- Crafts
- Lite Brite
- Lacing toys
- Sneaky, Snacky Squirrel Game!
- Perfection
- Hi Ho! Cherry-O
- Mr. Potato Head
- LEGO sets
- Design and Drill

A FINAL WORD

. . . .

We have made it to the end of our journey through the sensory system. Although we just scratched the surface, what you have learned is plenty to help your child develop and thrive. I truly believe that understanding a child's sensory system not only impacts how we think about them as learners but also influences their behaviors and guides us on how to best support them. When I meet a child, whether I am at work or not (I can't turn it off), I immediately notice what's going on with their sensory system and adjust my responses and expectations accordingly. Behavior is communication, and no two kids react the same way or need the same kind of support, sensory input, and parenting. I hope this book helped you to better understand your own child and how their sensory systems contribute to their development.

If I could leave you with just one takeaway, it would be to remember to play. Like, really *play*. Get up and engage the senses. Don't worry about keeping up with the Joneses and the high-tech toys that beep and blink in their kids' hands; jump in that puddle instead. Clothes can be washed. The memories and the neural connections you will build by playing with—and, yes, getting messy with—your child are so much more valuable than any pair of pants. Give both of you permission to enjoy the freedom of exploring your backyard, going on hikes, pretending you are fighting snakes in the Amazon, building a pillow fort. Let your child play the way we did—it doesn't get much better than that. While the sensory activities in this book will allow your child to better navigate their world, I hope that playing with them has brought out your inner child, and, even more so, built a stronger connection between the two of you.

Whether you are playing an activity in this book or one of your own, give your child room to grow and learn from their mistakes. Be a safety net and not a cage. Love your little one while also letting them go. If they have an idea, allow them to give it a try, even if you are pretty sure it won't work. Give them the opportunity to find that out for themselves. Figuring things out, getting messy, and chasing new experiences will benefit them in the end.

Remember, we are all different. Perfect is not only boring; it doesn't exist. Embrace your child's quirks and turn them into strengths. How many times have I mentioned my own sensory system and personal quirks? I am thankful for those sensory needs; I wouldn't be here without them. While honoring and building the areas that need extra love, remember that we all have strengths and weaknesses, and make sure your child knows it, too.

Most of all, never forget that you are an incredible parent. Stop comparing yourself to other parents, because their child is not your child. You picked up this book to understand how your child develops, which means that you're already going above and beyond, and that counts. It says so much about who you are as a caregiver. Your kids are lucky to have you. You got this.

And when in doubt—just play.

APPENDIX
ALLIE'S FAVORITE THINGS

- Animagnets by Play 2 Progress
- Wooden push toys
- Wood Velcro fruit
- Simple baby play gym
- Manhattan Toy Company Skwish
- Scooter board
- Containers for container play
- Baby Paper
- Calmies
- Sophie the Giraffe
- Hape Scoot-Around
- Dolls
- Weighted stuffed animals
- Balance bike
- Wooden balance board
- Squigz
- Baby mirror
- Wooden musical instruments
- Peanut ball
- BOSU ball
- River stones
- Bilibo
- Body sock
- Tegu Tiles
- Moon sand
- Clay
- Empty boxes
- The Nugget
- Weighted balls
- Wikki Stix
- Mr. Bubble Foam Soap
- Costumes
- Pikler Triangle
- Pikler Arch
- Theraputty

- Exercise bands
- Stretchy String Fidget
  (Monkey Noodle)
- Chew toppers for
  the pencil

- Chewelry necklaces
- Tangle Brain Tools

ACKNOWLEDGMENTS

This book would not have been possible without a team surrounding me with cheers and love. I never thought that I, the child who struggled to learn to read, would be writing a book. I would not be here without many teachers and mentors who believed in me along the way, starting in kindergarten with Mrs. O'Connell from Ealy Elementary. We have long lost touch, but I hope that one day this book reaches you because the mark you left on my life is one that I will never forget. You saw my strengths instead of my weaknesses and never doubted what I could accomplish. A good kindergarten teacher lays the foundation for schooling, and I am lucky to have had the best.

Jean Ayres and every OT that has come before me, who shaped the field of sensory integration into what it is today. Without your work, I would not get to live my passion. Renee, who read the book and pushed me to make it better. I appreciate everything.

Nina and the entire team at TarcherPerigee, for believing in this book and making it a reality. Jane and Karen, from Aevitas, who guided me along the way. Sheila, this book would not have been possible without you. My Friday mornings could not have started off in a better way. Thank you for everything.

To our P2P community, who fills our hallways with laughs and trusts us in the most difficult moments. I feel incredibly lucky that we get to watch so many kids grow up and help guide you through this wild journey of parenthood.

To our team at P2P, I could never properly express my gratitude for each one of you. Thank you for holding the space for parents, pushing every creative limit, creating a team atmosphere that is one in a million, and of course, for the fun! You are the best!

Brian, the artist behind every illustration and also an incredible friend. You made this book come alive.

Dad, I have no doubt you are looking down and smiling. You gave me the spark of curiosity, taught me to never stop learning and that the answer is not always right in front of you, but if you keep searching you will find it. I am saving a copy with your name on it!

Mom, my fierce cheerleader who truly believes there are no limits to what I can accomplish. Thank you for always being in my corner, for never letting anyone doubt me and always allowing me to explore— even when that meant taking apart everything in the house to see how it worked. I know it wasn't easy, but I appreciate it all.

Hayley, my sister and partner in kitchen spin competitions and living-room dance parties. I was lucky to have a big sister who was always willing to join me in getting all the sensory input we needed, right in the middle of the kitchen, and who taught me the ins and outs of life all before bed. Without you, I would never have made it through my first day of kindergarten, and that was only the first big day you helped guide me through.

Allison, my best friend, business partner, and soul sister. Few people are lucky enough to have a friendship as special as ours, but even fewer get to create something amazing with that friend. This book would never have been finished without your knowing exactly how to complete my thoughts, encouraging me, and reading along the way. I could say thank you 1,111 times and it still would not be enough.

Candace and Charles, my life changed the day I answered your Sittercity message. Thank you for seeing something in me before I saw it in myself, believing in me and always mentoring me along the way. There is no way I could express in words how thankful I am for you and your two perfect (okay, almost perfect) boys.

Lastly, to JJ and Asher, my nephews who inspire me to always continue playing. I love you endlessly and feel so lucky that I get to be your aunt.

NOTES

Introduction: Sensory Success

xi **If a child constantly wore mittens:** S. A. Cermack and L. A. Daunhauer, "Sensory Processing in the Postinstitutionalized Child," *The American Journal of Occupational Therapy* 51, no. 7(July–August 1997): 500–07.

xvi **We all know that we should cut down:** John S. Hutton, et al., "Associations Between Screen-Based Media Use and Brain White Matter Integrity in Preschool-Aged Children," *JAMA Pediatrics* 174, no. 1(2020): e193869, doi:10.1001/jamapediatrics.2019.3869, https://jamanetwork.com /journals/jamapediatrics/article-abstract/2754101.

Chapter 1: The Sensory System

1 **Although we can continue to improve our sensory system:** "Why the First 5 Years of Child Development Are So Important," Children's Bureau blog, https://www.all4kids.org/news/blog/why-the-first-5-years-of-child -development-are-so-important/.

6 **Jean Ayres, an occupational therapist:** A. Jean Ayres, *Sensory Integration and Learning Disorders* (Los Angeles: Western Psychological Services, 1972).

11 **It also influences their ability to identify:** Kelly Mahler, "What Is Interoception?," accessed December 28, 2019, https://www.kelly-mahler .com/what-is-interoception.

14 **Not all toys are created equal:** Anna V. Sosa, "How Does Type of Toy Affect Quantity, Quality of Language in Infant Playtime?," *JAMA Pediatrics*, December 23, 2015, https://media.jamanetwork.com/news -item/how-does-type-of-toy-affect-quantity-quality-of-language-in -infant-playtime.

Chapter 5: Seeing Clearly

117 **We want to see those inconsistencies:** Kate Kelly, "FAQS About Reversing Letters, Writing Letters Backwards, and Dyslexia," https://www .understood.org/en/learning-thinking-differences/child-learning

-disabilities/dyslexia/faqs-about-reversing-letters-writing-letters-backwards
-and-dyslexia.

Chapter 6: A Little Taste

138 **This is one of the reasons why it is critical:** Julie A. Mennella, Coren P. Jagnow, and Gary K. Beauchamp, "Prenatal and Postnatal Flavor Learning by Human Infants," *Pediatrics* 107, no. 6(June 2001): E88, https://www .ncbi.nlm.nih.gov/pmc/articles/PMC1351272.

139 **It can take many times:** Julie A. Mennella, "Ontogeny of Taste Preferences: Basic Biology and Implications for Health," *American Journal of Clinical Nutrition* 99, no. 3(March 2014): 704S—711S, https://pubmed .ncbi.nlm.nih.gov/24452237.

140 **the signals combine with other sensory information:** Institute for Quality and Efficiency in Health Care, "How Does Our Sense of Taste Work?," National Center for Biotechnology Information, December 20, 2011, last updated August 17, 2016, https://www.ncbi.nlm.nih.gov/books /NBK279408.

141 **Because taste preferences start even before birth:** Mariya Voytyuk, "Food Preferences," 2016, https://scholar.googleusercontent.com/scholar?q =cache:tHMNgRpUeAIJ:scholar.google.com/&hl=en&as_sdt=0,5.

Chapter 7: Scent-sational

152 **Among the first scents we encounter are those of our moms:** Shota Nishitani, et al., "The Calming Effect of a Maternal Breast Milk Odor on the Human Newborn Infant," *Neuroscience Research* 63, no. 1(2009): 66–71, http://naosite.lb.nagasaki-u.ac.jp/dspace/bitstream/10069/20844/9 /NeuRes63_66_text.pdf.

152 **Our sense of smell is the one:** Colleen Walsh, "What the Nose Knows," *Harvard Gazette*, February 27, 2020, https://news.harvard.edu/gazette /story/2020/02/how-scent-emotion-and-memory-are-intertwined-and -exploited.

154 **From there, the signal is passed to:** "How Smell Works," Fifth Sense, accessed June 18, 2020, https://www.fifthsense.org.uk/how-smell-works-2.

154 **When an infant is born:** Jennifer M. Cernoch and Richard H. Porter, "Recognition of Maternal Axillary Odors by Infants," *Child Development* 56 (1985): 1593–98, http://faculty.weber.edu/eamsel/Classes/Child %203000/Assignments/Assign%201/recognition.pdf.

154 **We have the ability to identify tons:** "Taste and Smell," in Charles Molnar and Jane Gair, *Concepts of Biology: 1st Canadian Edition*, 2015, w opentextbc.ca/biology/chapter/17-3-taste-and-smell.

154 **Think about the last time:** Mass. Eye and Ear Communications, "More Than Taste Buds," *Focus* (blog), June 11, 2018, https://focus.masseyeandear .org/more-than-taste-buds-how-smell-influences-taste.

Chapter 8: Sounds Good!

165 **By the end of the pregnancy, they will:** Kristin M. Voegtline, et al., "Near-Term Fetal Response to Maternal Spoken Voice," *Infant Behavior and Development* 36, no. 4(2013): 526–33, https://www.ncbi.nlm.nih.gov /pmc/articles/PMC3858412.

Chapter 9: The Sense Inside the Body

182 **The signals created by these receptors:** Michelle Colletti, "The Creation of Emotion: The Journey from Interoception to Embodied Self-Awareness," Elite Healthcare, May 8, 2019, https://www.elitecme.com /resource-center/rehabilitation-therapy/the-creation-of-emotionthe -journey-from-interoception-to-embodied-self-awareness.

182 **There isn't much research on the development of interoceptive:** Lara Maister, Teresa Tang, and Manos Tsakiris, "Neurobehavioral Evidence of Interoceptive Sensitivity in Early Infancy," eLife, August 8 2017, https:// elifesciences.org/articles/25318.

182 **Recent studies have also examined how interoception:** ADVANCE Staff, "Interoception: The Eighth Sensory System," Elite Healthcare, May 27, 2016, https://www.elitecme.com/resource-center/rehabilitation-therapy /interoception-the-eighth-sensory-system.

INDEX

Entries in bold refer to specific activities.

ABOUT THE AUTHOR

. . . .

Allie's mission is to empower children and their families through sensory play so that they can thrive through childhood and beyond. Allie uses the science of child development and the joy of play to boost children's confidence and enhance development within all areas of their life, from social and emotional to physical and academic. Allie believes that the best way to support children is by arming their parents, from inception, with the knowledge and skills necessary to encourage their child's development for success through childhood and beyond.

Allie began her work in pediatric development at the University of Michigan, where she earned her bachelor's degree in

Movement Science, and continued her studies at University of Southern California, where she received her master's and clinical doctorate in Occupational Therapy. Allie is certified in Sensory Integration and hopes that one day quality open-ended play will be considered as important as learning the ABC's.

ABOUT PLAY 2 PROGRESS

Play 2 Progress is a popular play-based learning platform that helps all kids build the key developmental skills they need to succeed. With two locations in the Los Angeles area, a virtual studio, and a developmental toy line, Play 2 Progress uses the science of child development coupled with the joy of play to help kids thrive in all areas of their lives by simply doing what they do best—play! Play 2 Progress also offers classes for parents to educate, empower, and guide them on the journey through parenthood—from pregnancy through preschool and beyond.